HOW
TO
Barter

&Trade

by
JACK TRAPP

CORNERSTONE LIBRARY
PUBLISHED BY SIMON & SCHUSTER, NEW YORK

Published by Cornerstone Library, Inc.
A Simon & Schuster Division of
Gulf & Western Corporation
Simon & Schuster Building
1230 Avenue of the Americas
New York, New York 10020

CORNERSTONE LIBARY and colophon are trademarks of
Simon & Schuster, registered in the U.S. Patent and Trademark Office.

Manufactured in the United States of America
10 9 8 7 6 5 4 3 2 1

ISBN 0-346-12483-2

2162113

Contents

Author's Note

For 20 years I have been a full-time freelance writer and have written over 100 books in the fields of home remodeling, gardening, crafts, and so on. In all my books, and especially in the ones about gardening, I have stressed the advantages of self-sufficiency. Indeed, one was originally titled the *Gardener's Guide to Survival* but was subsequently retitled by an editor who felt that was too strong a handle.

In my work I have had contacts with craftsmen, gardeners, remodelers, contractors, and carpenters, and I have seen life-styles changing drastically over the past decades. Recently, the self-sufficiency movement has been given paramount billing, and rightfully so, and since many of my neighbors started bartering some time ago, I joined in. Bartering is inherent in the survival kit, and I found it to be the missing link in my own life chain.

I have written books on building your own house, books on growing food, and other self-help books. These I believe offer the key to survival in a chaotic world that seems to be getting worse daily—self-help or how-to information in various areas. In that world, bartering is the natural form of order, and, I believe today, a very real and important part of the future.

Introduction: Supply and Demand

You may think you cannot get along without more money; you may think that inflation is going to scuttle your ship and doomsday is around the corner. If you do believe the great crash is on the way, you better get ready to cash in on it without cash. You can do it—if you start to learn to barter and trade right now. There is nothing new about bartering—what's new is that it is becoming necessary again, as it was in great-grandma's time. Bartering is simply trading—one thing for another (a service or an item). It is growing every day in individual communities due to people like you and me. The flea market of the early '70s and the swap shops and co-ops have resurfaced, but in another—and better—way.

What bartering amounts to today is to create a neighborhood nucleus—a clearinghouse for services that can be offered by members and a list of things that normally cost dollars that are available. Swap, barter, trade, horse trade—call it what you will, but it saves money.

If you don't want to join one of the neighborhood set-ups, you can even barter on your own—individual to individual—and still save bucks.

In addition to neighborhood projects and person-to-person bartering, there are national bartering organizations throughout the country—hundreds of them—that act as clearinghouses to match want with need. Some charge membership fees while others do not, but instead work on a small percentage of the transaction—usually 10 percent. Thus, no cash changes hands between barterer and trader.

There is a host of people who have something to offer, whether it be typing or painting, decorating or gardening, or landscaping. And there are other people who may have things you want. The idea is to match "what you have" with "what you need." In this book you will find the methods, means, and how-to's of getting what you need without spending money. You do not have to be in business, be an entrepreneur or a lawyer. All you have to know is what you can supply that other people need and how to get what you need in exchange.

It all adds up to the only logical and sure way to beat inflation.

Barter can return you to the time when people felt safe with each other and with their own worth. They worked, traded, and prospered. Then, there was little concern about high energy consumption, soaring unemployment, and material shortages and strikes. These are the vanguards of our times, and hardly very happy experiences. Experts tell us this is bound to continue in force through the '80s—to what?

There must be some alternative to the frightening, harrowing existence most people find themselves in now. And there is. It is called *barter*. It worked for our forebears, and can and does work for us.

Barter is the best and most practical way of trading things or practices so you can get what you need without cash and without owing money through credit. You will have to barter if money becomes just paper, as it might. You can get needed and scarce commodities through bartering, secure collectibles as investments, decrease capital gains, redistribute assets, and trade talents to gain experience. It is a people's way of survival.

There are three basic bartering arrangements: services for goods, goods for goods, and services for services, and within these forms, there are endless possibilities to consider.

1 Why Barter?

The experts keep telling us a depression is just around the corner and price controls are inevitable. What with the high inflation rate, one is prone to believe these predictions. It does seem—even to the layperson—that the writing is on the wall, and so prudent people should think carefully and come to only one conclusion: it *can* happen.

In time of depression or inflation, barter traditionally becomes popular because it is the only logical way to get what you need for what you can offer. Money becomes worthless, but commodities become "money." It has happened before and can happen again.

During recessionary times, simple everyday items like toilet paper, cigarettes, whiskey, aspirin, flour, salt, and sugar become extremely valuable. This happened in European cities in 1945, when cigarettes were the prime trading currency. In Rome, two cigarettes

15

"bought" a great deal, and in Vienna a carton could buy a camera. In Berlin cigarettes were *the* currency. Charles Morrow Wilson, in his 1960 book *Let's Try Barter,* says a great deal about why it could happen and how it did happen.

INFLATION

Inflation is obviously the forerunner of barter—it has happened before and seems to be happening again as the inflation index rises week by week and month by month. And if wage and price controls come into effect, as some experts agree they will, bartering may be the only way to survive. In his good book, *Price Controls* (American Bureau of Economic Research), Gary North presents a frightening portrait of what may happen if wage and price controls are put into effect.

There are many guidebooks now to tell you how to cope with inflation by buying gold, silver, or investing in real estate, and so on. This is fine and it all may work as a hedge against inflation. However, most of us do not have sufficient funds to engage in these survival tactics. In order to buy whatever you need, you must have money—a good deal of it. For the majority of people, this is beyond their financial limits. But barter is not.

True, you won't make millions by bartering, but at least you can learn to survive and not find yourself out of cash when you come to the checkout counter. The authors of the many books on coupon trading are on the right track. Trading allows you to save big bucks, as well, and two very good books to look at are *Cashing in at the Cashout* (Stonesong Press) and *Guide to Cou-*

pons and Refunds (Bantam Books). For our purposes there are better ways (with bartering) to survive the coming years than trying to amass fortunes by buying gold, silver, diamonds, or real estate. We will discuss trading coupons in a future chapter.

Because a self-balancing exchange works in inflationary periods or under wage and price controls, this book tell you how to barter and what to barter. We dig deep to find what you have to offer and how you can profit by bartering—or, better yet, how you can live *without* cash.

BARTER BACKGROUND

Years ago bartering was for either the very rich or the very poor. It was thought of as demeaning by the middle classes, who had been taught to put their trust in hard cash. But times have certainly changed; now hard cash is becoming less an auspicious way of dealing in an economy where the dollar is worth much less than it was a decade ago. And it is the middle class who are hit the hardest when things go bad because they pay the lion's share of the taxes.

When there simply is no more money coming in, when the salaries of a household no longer can support the family, barter is the only answer. Credit is only for those who can afford it; some supplemental means of securing what you need (in addition to your paycheck) must be put into effect, and barter is that means.

You need not go all out into barter; you can keep it simple. Practice it occasionally to help you get along and to save cash. The benefits are many, as you will note in the following pages. The idea is to get out of the

habit of reaching for your wallet or credit card, a tough
habit to break since we have been conditioned for years
to believe that the more you spend, the better it is. But
it is better *for them*, not you!

Barter enables you to get what you need without
owing money. The practice is sound. According to early
American textbooks, student bills at Harvard could be
"paid" with produce and livestock. In times when currency was looked on with skepticism and people printed
their own money, it depreciated in value so fast that it
was always questionable, whereas a pig was not, nor
was a load of groceries.

BARTER IN OTHER NATIONS

You can go all the way back to Mesopotamia and to the
Romans to find that barter worked very well. The
Phoenicians, were leading traders of their time. Primi-
tive societies used barter extensively; obviously, they
had to because there was no "money" then as we know
it now. Sea shells, feathers, plants, and the like were
exchanged, with animals being perhaps the number-one
currency of the time. And the bazaars of Europe were
originally trade fairs, where goods were exchanged
swiftly and with a good deal of bargaining involved.
Money was not used—you horse-traded a swap or exchange, getting what you wanted in exchange for something you no longer needed. It all worked very well.

2 What Barter Is All About

Most likely you have bartered without even having been aware of it. For example, if you were invited to dinner at a friend's home and then later reciprocated by inviting that person to your home for dinner, you bartered. Maybe you sat with your neighbor's child while your neighbor picked up groceries for you while she or he was out on an errand—you both bartered services. Or perhaps you traded—bartered—a piece of furniture in exchange for some books. There are other, countless ways you have unconsciously bartered; learn to *consciously* barter for the necessities of life so you can afford to live better: for your vacation; for part of your rent; for fresh garden vegetables. Learn to live without reaching for cash all the time!

WHY BARTER WORKS

Simply put, bartering works because it reduces the amount of cash you need to live on. It gives you exactly what you need without using money.

Bartering can function to help you:

1. Limit or stop using credit cards
2. Save on taxes
3. Not worry about inflation
4. Save cash flow
5. Get exactly what you want and not just what stores offer
6. Meet new people
7. Integrate with social and ecological matters
8. To have fun

Bartering also helps you to:

1. Reuse articles
2. Recyle furniture and other items
3. Regenerate old items
4. Utilize time to the utmost when you deal in services
5. Accumulate antiques or collectibles

Bartering is a self-sustaining way of dealing and coping with the world as it is today. It puts you back in the driver's seat and makes you the boss of your own life. You need not depend on or worry about stores or shortages. A good barterer can get most essentials through trading in one area or another. And if you barter well, you get *exactly* what you want; you do not have to settle for second-best at stores.

Barter works because it makes good sense and is an individualistic approach to living rather than a cumulative monetary route to the poorhouse. If you think this is all idealistic talk, consider what the dollar buys today as compared to five years ago. When a loaf of bread sells for $5, and it might in the next few years (as it did in other inflation-plagued countries in the 1930s, when people with bushels of paper money could not even buy enough groceries for a week), you will understand why bartering just may be the only alternative we have. So get ready, just in case, and know how to barter to survive.

ROOTS OF BARTER

As we mentioned previously, bartering was practiced extensively throughout the world for centuries. Its renaissance was in the 1960s, when the flower children began the "back to the earth" movement. Their culture thrived on flea markets and exchanging time or services; indeed, many flower children survived only by bartering. And in their process the rest of us truly became aware of our environment, our resources.

A prime motive for this back-to-nature concept was a desire and a need to shed the yoke of government bureaucracy and yet, survive. The hippies started communes whose impetus was the concept of sharing and a general awareness of each other. Many of these communes worked well, and today some still survive. They work on a trade or sharing basis. But in the 1970s we developed an attitude of "me-ism"; everyone looks out for Number 1—himself or herself. But now, in the 1980s, this attitude is changing. Again we are caring about our environment and neighbors because we know that a fair amount of sharing and giving is the only way to survive both individually and collectively as a nation.

Many people have learned that it is possible to be self-sufficient, that they can live with less cash, that there are ways to cope. Bartering is back in style and seems to be well on its way to becoming an intelligent way of life.

SERVICES YOU CAN BARTER

If you think you do not have any worthwhile goods or services, think again. There are innumerable ways you can trade and get what you want without actually using money. Consider the following true examples:

A potter who lives in San Francisco takes his work around the city twice a month. Rather than trying to actually sell his work, which would entail having a place of business, a license, sales tax, overhead, and so on, he trades his craftwares for clothing, food, and even art supplies. He is able to do this because through the years he has kept a list of acquaintances and friends who have something he wants and who want what he has to offer.

An interior designer moved into a new home in the city and needed kitchen appliances. She established a contact within a local appliance company in that city and was about to buy appliances on time when she discovered that the store was moving to new headquarters and needed interior design services. She did the designing and was "paid" in appliances.

One young woman was so talented at sewing that she could make almost any item of clothing. Down the road from her lived a couple with six children and a large garden and some cattle stock. Cynthia, fond of fresh produce and meat, made a deal to furnish one article of

clothing for each child in exchange for free use of the
garden and a supply of beef; thus, she got fresh produce
and meat all year long (more about bartering services in
Chapter 7).

You are now probably grumbling and thinking:
"Fine, those people have talent—but what can I
offer?" Think harder. True, you may not have artistic
skills, but no doubt you have other skills or items to
exchange, or at least time—time to care for children,
house-sit, watch plants, answer phones, and so forth.
There are a host of things you can trade without having
specialized skills. It is just a matter of finding out what
you can do to get what you want and save money.

For example, here is a partial list of services and
commodities you can barter, trade, or exchange:

Services
• Architecture
• Baby-sitting
• Calligraphy
• Carpentry
• Car-pooling
• Catering
• Coaching
• Editing
• Electrical work
• Gardening
• Interior decorating
• Landscape design
• Painting
• Plumbing
• Stenography
• Tutoring
• Typing

Commodities
- Antiques
- Books
- Clothing
- Collectibles
- Crafts
- Food
- Furniture
- Machinery
- Tools
- Vacations

However, do not think you can fulfill all life's necessities and save all your money by bartering. It is not a total panacea for inflation, but it is a substantial start. In other words, if nothing else, let bartering help you keep up with inflation. After you get your feet wet, you may want to try and balance the books by using bartering as a way of life. Start slowly, take your time, and have fun. Yes, you will have fun—because you will be meeting lots of people, most of them very nice and quite like you. The one big factor we all have in common is trying to survive financially in an inflated world in which money is becoming less and less money, and more and more just *paper*.

3 Getting Started: How to Do It, and Pitfalls to Avoid

To barter you must find the person who has what you want for what you can offer in exchange. At first it will seem difficult to find such a person, but if you approach bartering in an organized and sensible way, you will find your contacts. A form of bartering exists among realtors, politicians, lobbyists, freelancers, and so on —you will be bartering on a smaller scale, but you, too, can establish valuable networks if you do a little planning. You can start very basically by trading on a one-to-one basis. This basic form of bartering is easy to do, involves no hassle, and is very popular. However, you cannot exist solely on this kind of bartering; it is strictly a supplement to your basic income. It can save dollars, but to really get involved in bartering, you should try to build a bigger foundation.

There are six basic ways to find your barter partner:

1. Word of mouth (neighborhood groups)
2. Notices on supermarket or office bulletin boards
3. Newspaper and magazine ads
4. Barter clubs
5. Exchanges and networks
6. Swap meets and trade fairs.

WORD OF MOUTH: NEIGHBORHOOD GROUPS

This is a logical extension of the basic one-to-one bartering method. Word of mouth is essentially a neighborhood method and can work effectively on a house-to-house basis. First, it is absolutely necessary that you know your neighbors. This thought may frighten you, especially if you crave privacy, but if you want to barter, you better get friendlier. And you may be pleasantly surprised—bartering leads to a help-thy-neighbor attitude.

Know your neighbors' skills and assess their attitudes about sharing and their honesty in carrying out a transaction. Do not ring doorbells unannounced or barge in on your neighbors; instead, phone ahead, introduce yourself, and ask your neighbors if they would be interested in a neighborhood barter club. (God knows that if Tupperware has made it through this routine, you can, too!) Carefully explain bartering to them, or offer them this book. Tell your neighbors what you have to trade, ask what they might have, and determine if they would be interested in swapping.

To ease your beginnings, start with friends first, and then advance to other neighbors. If there is enough goodwill, with minimum effort you can make not only financial gains, but emotional ones as well by getting to know your neighbors. Ask simple questions, like: "What skills do you have?," "What do you need most?," and "What chores would you like to cooperate in?" This way you will naturally set up a bartering framework. You can extend the framework by having house parties, with each neighbor in turn hosting a get-together for participants to discuss what they have and what they want.

The word-of-mouth neighborhood bartering plan works better than you may think: it allows you to know your neighbors and to actually see what you are getting; it establishes a personal one-for-all-and-all-for-one attitude that generally avoids any arguments or dissension; and it is perhaps the wisest way of getting what you need without laying out cash.

NOTICES ON SUPERMARKET OR OFFICE BULLETIN BOARDS

Bulletin boards in supermarkets and your office always post notices about gardening, house-cleaning, baby-sitting, things for sale, and so on. Tack up your own cards, listing what items or services you have available or what you want. State clearly on your notice that you are offering a bartering service, with *no money* exchanging hands, and list the phone contact. (At work you will have the advantage of being able to actually know or talk directly to an interested "barterer." And at work, word of mouth is always going on.)

You will get calls, so be ready. Have cards on hand on which to list the name of the person calling, what he or she is offering, and his or her phone number. If you cannot use their services or items, you might be able to mix and match them with someone you know who does have what they want or needs what they are trying to exchange.

If you get enough calls and people check out okay (you can usually tell this by talking to callers for a while), you might set up a bartering party at your house to get acquainted. Remember, nothing ventured, nothing gained.

Local notices and ads can also be put up at church and at schools where these are allowed. Investigate all facets; call to find out if such notices are allowed.

NEWSPAPER AND MAGAZINE ADS

Swap ads and exchange ads appear in small newspapers in the classified section. You can place an ad for about $2. Clearly and explicitly list what you have to exchange or what you need. When answers come in by phone, be ready with index cards and list all pertinent information.

Local newspaper ads are great for exchange vacation rentals, art or piano lessons for children, and other services; they are not so good for food or furniture, however.

The "earth" magazines of the 1970s began to serve as a clearinghouse for bartering and swap ads, with *Mother Earth News* perhaps being the most popular. Here you can trade any item; from a piece of land to a house trailer to a gross of zucchini. Or you can exchange your services, such as working on a farm for free room and board. The gamut of ads in this magazine and others is incredible and covers almost all the essential things one needs to survive.

For years such magazines have been extolling the virtues of going back to nature, making it on your own, and leading a self-sufficient life. Bartering is definitely one of their credos, and judging from the amount of ads such magazines carry, the enterprise is quite successful.

Generally the ads are minimal in cost, and you can establish a whole life-style around the bartering concept by placing ads about your wants or needs or what you have to offer and would like to get rid of.

Other magazines expressly for traders include the *Great Exchange*, available for $12 a year, 655 Madison Ave., New York, N.Y. 10021, and *Barter Communiqué*, a newspaper published twice a year for $1 a copy and available from Full Circle Marketing Corp., 6500 Midnight Pass Rd., Penthouse Suite #504, Sarasota, Fla. 33581.

BARTER CLUBS & EXCHANGE NETWORKS

Of special interest is the Comstock Trading Company. This organization offers a full barter program and issues a magazine called the *Trading Post*, filled with practical barter advice and thousands of ads for possible trades of all kinds of goods and services; this magazine is issued every month to members. In addition, there is a special report called the *Comstock Quarterly*, with comprehensive investment and trading opportunities for an alternative economy. Also included with a membership fee is a "yellow page" directory divided into 150 separate categories, like accounting, art, and so on. To get this information, you must become a member of the company, which entails a yearly fee. Write directly to the Comstock Trading Company, P. O. Box 8020, Walnut Creek, Calif. 94596.

We discuss barter clubs and exchanges in greater detail in future chapters.

SWAP MEETS AND TRADE FAIRS

The swap meet is becoming very popular, appearing in many outlying towns. For years several counties have had monthly swap meets or trade fairs, like those in Texas and California. But now the smaller meet is popular, and here is an ideal place to get rid of something you do not want for something you do want. The items I have seen at swap meets run from toy trains to bathroom lavatories. There is incredible variety and incredible fun in seeing what is available. Many times you will discover that hard-to-find wicker chair at a swap meet —if you have something to trade for it. Grandma's old cookbooks might be just the ticket if you feel ready to get rid of them.

Generally, swap meets and trade fairs are listed in local newspapers or magazines. They are either a monthly event or occur only during the spring and summer. Look for them. Make contact and get yourself a space at such meetings. It is a great way to spend a Sunday and a great place to find things and unload those things you want to get rid of. There is great value in used furniture for functional reasons, let alone the savings in money. And often at these trading places you can find items you have searched for for years. I was lucky enough to locate a great old bird cage at one such Sunday fair, and since I collect cages, that was quite a find, indeed.

Trade fairs are becoming increasingly popular in rural areas, and in some cities there are monthly trade fairs similar to flea markets where an array of items is offered for trade. These are excellent places to find that out-of-the-way piece of furniture or a clock you want or kitchen appliances, and so forth. In addition to meeting new people and having some fun, you in turn can offer things you don't use anymore. It's an ideal way to find a new owner for Aunt Tillie's last Christmas gift.

Watch local newspapers for notices of trade fairs in your area. Local organizations many times have information on fairs, as well.

HOW TO BARTER

There are really no set rules on how to barter and I can only make some suggestions to help you. Most people are genuinely good horse traders and swappers—they seem to know naturally how to get what they want in exchange for something they don't want. Here are some helpful hints to get you a-bartering:

1. Never appear too anxious, but show genuine interest.
2. Exchange good or services at the same time—when you give your commodity, try to get back what you want at the same time or a reasonable length of time thereafter.
3. If the value of your service or goods is more than the going value of what you are getting—don't argue. Accept a straight trade rather than getting into a hassle.
4. If you are writing a barter ad for a magazine or paper, be very specific. Don't hedge.
5. If you are bartering for collectibles, know your "thing"—and know it well. This applies to antiques, books, stamps, Oriental rugs, clocks, and other collectibles.

6. If you do get into real estate exchanges be sure to have a lawyer help you. Barter for his or her services.
7. In the exchange of goods, remember that there are no guarantees, and if that old refrigerator you got in exchange for an old TV set goes haywire, forget about making a complaint.

BARTERER BEWARE

There are many items that can be bartered, as we discussed, and most exchanges of goods and services work out fine, but there are some pitfalls I strongly urge you to avoid.

Used Cars

Trying to select a used car on an open lot is chancy in itself; trying to barter something for a used car is like trying to look into a crystal ball, because you never know what you may get. If you trade for a lemon, you have no recourse. Stay away from used-car bartering!

Real Estate

There is really no need to elaborate upon the many nefarious land deals that have occurred in the past few decades; many people were stuck with useless land because swamps were advertised as suburbs and deserts as tropical havens. There certainly are reliable land deals, but there are also some very dubious ones, so I suggest you avoid bartering for land.

Jewelry

To barter jewelry wisely, you must be almost an expert. You simply cannot take the word of a would-be barterer that the diamonds or the emeralds are genuine. The particular owner may not know, and you certainly would not know unless you are qualified.

Stolen Goods

Can this happen in bartering? Yes, it sure can, but not on the large scale one might think. Generally, when bartering with friends or people you know, this simply does not happen, but when bartering on the larger collective market, such as in flea markets, it is possible, so be cautious.

PRECAUTIONS

If you are bartering on a large scale and in many areas, consulting experts in a specific field is a wise idea. Camera trading goes on frequently in the United States, and yet this is an area where you must really know your product. Read, talk to other people who have similar cameras, even go to your local camera store and seek out information. Talk is free, and most people behind sales counters will talk. But try not to get the owner of the store.

If you are into collectibles and antiques, I suggest you really know your stuff. Read the many periodicals on these subjects. These magazines are sold at local newsstands. Subscribe to papers that feature collect-

ibles, and have a good collectible book that lists prices.
(See Chapter 6 for more about antiques and collectibles,
crafts and tools.)

Paintings, whether early American or whatever, is
another area that demands shrewd bartering. Whether
you do this as a hobby or as a hedge against inflation,
know what you are talking about. Again, consult various art magazines and periodicals, talk to gallery people, and get a handle on values of going works by the
same artist you are bartering with.

Dealing in plants as exchange items also requires
some know-how. Get acquainted with plants by their
botanical names so you know what you are getting. For
example, a *Howiea kentia* palm retails for about $20 a
foot—that is, $80 for a four-foot plant, which is quite
expensive. A plant that resembles *Howiea,* called
Areca, retails for $7 a foot—quite a savings. But some-
times it is hard to tell the difference, so check mail-
order suppliers for prices and values and read their catalogs to learn how to identify plants.

Trading wood-working tools like saws takes a good
deal of expertise to determine just what you are getting.
Since you are dealing with used machinery, you can
end up on the short end of the stick if you are not
mechanically oriented and know your screws, rivets,
and other materials. This does not mean that the person
selling that band saw knows it is imperfect; machinery
just has a way of going out of whack at the least ex-
pected time. Study catalogs published by Penney's,
Ward's, and Sears for pricing, and read some books on
wood-working tools.

Appliance trading can be hazardous, but not half as
bad as trading automobiles. Trading a used or a surplus
range for a dishwasher, for example, can be okay, if

you know the person exchanging the item. You can save a great deal of cash, and if you are reasonably knowledgeable in the field you can determine the workings of small or large appliances.

In all trades and exchanges, ask questions. Ask why the person is making the trade, and ask how long the item was in service. Observe if the person is overanxious or in a hurry to complete the deal. Learn to trust your instincts, as well as your knowledge of an item.

DETERMINING VALUES

If you barter on a small scale, determining the value of an item or a service such as typing or photography generally is not a problem. A straight one-to-one trade can just be arranged by word of mouth, but not always; it depends on whom you are dealing with. For best results it is wise to know the value of the items and services we have discussed here, and then have some form of written agreement, be it only a slip of paper with signatures. The reason for these precautions is evident. After some time goes by, an individual may think he or she has been gypped and start hollering. Often verbal promises fall by the wayside, so something in writing to remind the parties involved is most helpful.

ITEMS

Can you *accurately* determine the monetary value of such items as clothing, food, furniture? With today's high rate of inflation, these prices are continually changing so drastically that it can be difficult to pinpoint the actual values. Yet there are guidelines you can follow. For example, for food prices, survey supermarket ads in newspapers. Know what vegetables are going for, and what preserves and such commodities as peanut butter that you can make at home are worth.

If you are dealing in furniture, make trips to local stores and establish a price list for end tables, planters, or whatever you want to trade or get in exchange. Keep the list simple, but up to date. If you are bartering with homemade clothing or want custom clothes, know what the retail stores are charging. Make notes and lists about blouses, skirts, shirts, slacks, and so on. Itemize each essential piece of clothing on a card.

SERVICES

When you barter for services like interior design or decorating, landscape gardening consultation, electrical or plumbing work, the problem of fair exchange is somewhat complex. True, you can call various firms and ask what their hourly prices are and make suitable lists, but often, because of unions and other factors, service prices are so astronomical that it would be facetious to think you can barter equally with items. And often it is hard to put a price on an "intellectual" skill. Bartering for services takes more time and talk than bartering one item for another. It can get complicated: Can you equally barter a simple homemade planter for an hour of intricate plumbing services? Or if you offer a professional service that goes for $21 per hour on the market, will what you get in return be worth that much? If you maintain the going price, the other person may just go elsewhere.

WRITTEN AGREEMENTS

If you are not acquainted with your barter partner (and sometimes even if you are), put down something in writing you both can sign so there is always an agreement on record. This can eliminate costly debates and arguments later; the signed papers need not be drawn up by attorneys. A simple note saying you are trading one chair for one blouse, with both signatures and the date, is usually all that is necessary.

If you start involving lawyers and notaries, you are defeating the purpose of bartering, and it will become more of a chore than a pleasure. The simple piece of paper reminding your partner that he or she agreed to the original barter is generally all that is needed.

The paper with signatures is also a good idea in case the I.R.S. questions a trade; then you have it in writing —all legal.

If you barter on a large scale in a club or neighborhood barter group, by all means have some proof of trade in writing, because the more you trade and the more you get in trade, the more prudent it is to have some records of these transactions. Remember that a signed piece of paper protects not only you, but your partner as well, so it should not be considered an insult, but just good sense.

4 The Big Three

If people had to list where the major part of their paycheck goes, it would break down into: housing (or rent),
clothing, and food. These are everyday expenditures
that must be met in one way or another, and they con-
sume the largest share of our money.

If you can barter or trade services or skills or labor
or what-have-you for part (or all) of your rent, you save
a pocketful of money. There are ways of doing this, but
it takes some know-how.

If you know people who sew, you can try to get some
clothing from them for yourself by finding something or
some service they require from you. Clothes cost big
money at stores—look to talented people in your neighborhood who can make them for you.

Food can also be bartered for: ads on bulletin boards
in supermarkets frequently turn up a harvest of produce
which can save you lots of money. And if you have a

vegetable garden, you can get many things you want because so many people are seeking untainted, unsprayed produce. Just securing fruits and vegetables for your family can cut your food budget drastically. Let's look at each of these money-eating commodities and see how to deal with them.

RENT

1. If you are seeking a new rental, look for larger buildings where you might become manager for all your rent, or at least part of it.

Often, landlords have a difficult time finding a trustworthy person, or in some states, housing laws require that a building manager be on the premises of more than a four-unit complex.

2. Offer your gardening services or maintenance services for part of, or all, your rent.

Most buildings have gardens, and someone has to maintain the grounds, small though they may be. Lobby, hall, and stairway cleaning are also necessary.

3. Offer bookkeeping services, especially if a landlord has more than one building, in exchange for part of your rent.

If a landlord has to have a rental agency to perform this service, it can run into big bucks.

4. If the landlord offers to paint or renovate your apartment, offer to do it yourself in exchange for a break in the rent for a month or two.

Today, union painters charge high prices, and the owner of the building may let you paint all the apartments in the complex.

5. Offer to lay carpet, wax or refinish floors, or any in-the-home craft in exchange for a portion of your rent.

These services are expensive when done by outside workers, and many times owners cannot find people to do the job when they want it done.

Any of the above methods can save you a bundle of money. *All you need do is ask*.

House Building

With all the books written on how to build your own home, it's a wonder there is a contractor still working. But building your own house by yourself is almost an impossibility; what makes the do-it-yourself house work is trade-off help. I have seen this concept work very well in California. Services were exchanged instead of money, and this makes good sense.

Some friends adept at carpentry traded their services for a roofer who needed some cabinet work done. When it came time to pour the foundation for the house, the couple offered their carpentry skills in exchange for this job. Eventually, through a joint effort with perhaps ten different people working on their house (including an electrician who wanted fresh produce and a plumber who wanted some handmade quilts), my friends got their house built with little hard cash. They bartered and exchanged services—and, yes, I ended up doing the landscaping for them (because that is one of my skills) in exchange for using the house in the hills for several weekends a year.

So if you want to build a house, get to know some people and start asking about trading services, but be prepared—you must have something to offer in return, whether it be produce or sewing or carpentry. Have an arsenal of bartering artillery on your side and you sure can build your own house. It isn't easy and it takes time —almost two years for the above couple's home to be completed—but they saved close to $25,000, and that ain't peanuts.

CLOTHING

With today's prices you can spend an entire weekly paycheck on only one piece of clothing. Why not invest in a handmade article which will always be distinctive and generally better made than a factory-produced item? To find a person who sews, consult ads on bulletin boards, or if you sew yourself, put your own card up on the bulletin board. When you are seeking clothing, you will find that perhaps a seamstress or tailor needs something in return—possibly your skills as a secretary, an editor, or interior decorator. You must ask to find out. Don't be timid—you can save dollars.

FOOD

You have only to look in the newspapers to know that food prices are highly inflated and getting worse by the day. The inflation rate of food prices is the highest it has ever been in this country. Whether it is a head of cauliflower or a pound of coffee, the cost of food is out of sight. But you can save as much as $1,000 a year by just growing vegetables in a ten-by-twenty-foot vegetable patch. Anyone who gardens knows that there is always too much zucchini, cauliflower, squash, and tomatoes ripening *at any one time*. Here, then, is an excellent way of getting rid of your surplus food: barter it for something you might need. Find out what the person has to offer and go after it.

If you do not have a garden:

1. Find someone who does and offer to help cultivate the garden in exchange for some produce.

Most gardeners generally have an abundance of vegetables because so many mature at the same time. Most gardeners can never get enough help in tending their gardens.

2. Inquire about community garden projects in your neighborhood; many urban areas now are engaged in this money-saving tactic.

In the community garden concept, you trade work for produce, or vice versa—everyone gets a piece of the action, and no money changes hands.

3. If you don't garden or don't want to, but still want to save money, offer to supply compost or fencing or whatever the gardener needs for the vegetable patch in order to obtain some produce for yourself.

Many gardeners have the land, but not the additional money for compost, soils, and plants.

4. If you do not know of anyone with a garden, ask

around or look for ads on bulletin boards in supermarkets—or put up your own ad.

Obviously, the main idea here is to save the exorbitant prices of produce in stores; but another very important factor is that you get fresh, untainted, unsprayed fruits and vegetables—far better for your health than mass-market goods.

If you want to start a garden yourself on your own land or have a friend who has land, here is a short course on vegetable farming for city or suburb.

Garden Guide

1. Good fertile soil is the key to a successful small garden.
2. Supplement existing soil with compost, manure, bonemeal.
3. Add topsoil to create a vitally alive soil. Compost is decayed organic matter. It adds nutrients and gives the soil a lighter texture, allowing the soil to "breathe," which is important so water can reach plant roots. You can make compost or buy it in tidy sacks.
4. To prepare the garden beds, break up and dig up the existing soil to a depth of at least 18 inches.
5. Once the soil is broken up, add topsoil.
6. Level the bed with a rake and then add a 2-inch layer of manure.
7. Turn ingredients just into the top portion of the soil and rake into a light texture.
8. Make planting rows and sow seeds or put in pre-started plants available from nurseries at seasonal times.

Watering

People know that to have produce, they must water their plants. But too often people do not realize just how much water plants need: vegetables and berries need bucketsful; herbs and fruit trees require somewhat less. How much is "bucketsful"? At least two hours' worth of watering every day in the hot months of June, July, and August. Soil should be uniformly moist at all times, because even some slight drying out can cause carrots to crack, beets to turn woody, radishes to get pithy, bean pods to shrivel, and cucumbers to give poor yields. Water is the lifeline of the vegetable patch. Use it.

An erratic watering schedule—such as one week of watering followed by three days of neglect—can also cripple food plants. Unlike annuals and perennials, which can tolerate this inconsistent treatment, vegetables cannot; the stop-and-start syndrome can ruin a crop.

Although it is true that food crops need lots of water, do not overdo the amount. Provide just enough water, never too much. Admittedly, this is tricky. What is too much? Too much is any amount that lets the soil get soggy enough so that air spaces are suffocated. Without oxygen entering the soil through air spaces, root growth stops; if this continues too long, plants die. This is why a very porous, loamy, almost fluffy soil is recommended: soil needs air.

So, to water correctly, *really* water the garden; scanty waterings do absolutely nothing. You must be sure that water penetrates the soil at least 20 inches (more is even better). How long does it take to water soil to this depth? If you have prepared the soil properly, it takes about 90 minutes. If you have poor soil (clayey or sandy), double the time.

If your vegetable garden is in containers, be sure that you water soil thoroughly here, also. You will have some clues as to when plants have enough water. Here's how to tell. Water the soil until excess water rains from the bottom of the planter or bin, and then water again to be sure all areas of the contained soil are uniformly moist. Most containers used for holding produce are large—tubs and boxes, for example—so do not treat the soil as you would for a pot plant. There is a vast difference in terms of vertical depth.

To sum up watering: when you water, water long and deep to plant roots so they really get moist. Try to keep soil evenly moist. Use a light application of general plant food every third week once plants are growing.

Harvesting

The trick is to harvest the vegetables when their flavor is at their peak. The best indicators of this ripe time are color and size. For example, eggplant should be picked when it is purple, yet before it loses its glossy shine; it should not be allowed to reach mammoth size. The same is true of squash, because the larger they grow, the less taste they have. Beets and carrots should be rather small when harvested. Again, the rule of thumb is to pick your barter bounty before it gets too large and get ready to trade surplus food.

STOCKING UP

Many books have been written on stocking up to save money, but buying canned or frozen foods to tide you over during a recession does not make good sense or cents. Canned foods have water in them, and their shelf life is not all that it is cracked up to be. Nutritional value of canned foods is low because of the heat used in the canning process. Nutritional value deteriorates long before food does.

Frozen food has an even shorter shelf life, and of course depends upon storage in freezers. In the event of catastrophic energy shortages (not so unthinkable), your frozen food will become useless. So fresh food is your best bet against inflation, and this means a garden of your own—grow your own. Not only will you be healthier for it (eating and doing it), but you will have great bartering power when you have stored food to offer. Can or dry food, package it, and squirrel it away. It could be the golden nugget for you when things get really rough. *Food is money in dire times*—it is the prime bartering artillery, so be prepared. Following is a short course on storing produce.

Facts About Storage

Most fruits and vegetables can be stored in any place where the temperature ranges between 32° and 40° F.; a few foods keep better at between 42° and 50° F. You yourself must provide the humidity for stored foods, because once they are picked they no longer get moisture from the original tree or plant. Most fruits and vegetables do fine at 80 to 90 percent humidity. Without proper humidity, stored foods will shrivel and lose their nutritional quality and color.

The ventilation within the storage area should be controlled, with neither too much nor too little air. Too much air will cause oxidation, which in turn will cause plants to decay. Light is not necessary to store foods. In fact, foods should be kept in darkness so the produce does not sprout. Some stored produce will last several

weeks, others several months. Later we will list lengths
of time for the storage of specific crops.

Foods can be stored in apple crates or wooden boxes
such as the ones fruits come to the supermarket in,
wood and plastic barrels, split-wood or plastic baskets,
even plastic bags. Make sure any container is scrupu-
lously clean and free of nails and staples. Do not use
very deep containers because too much produce piled
on top of itself can cause damage.

Preparing Produce for Storage

Here is a simple checklist to help you prepare your
foodstuffs for storage in the cellar, garage, pit or other
area:

1. Select only the choicest produce. Never store any food
   that has visible signs of decay or insect damage.
2. Wash the fruits and vegetables first, briskly and quickly.
   Handle the food as little as possible.
3. Harvest produce as late in the season as you can, but
   before the first frost.
4. Store only mature produce.
5. Never store any produce immediately after harvesting;
   allow it to sit overnight.
6. Do not store both fruits and vegetables together. Some
   fruits, such as apples and pears, give off ethylene gas,
   which causes carrots to taste bitter and tomatoes to ripen
   too quickly.
7. Do not put stored produce on concrete floors because concrete encourages the growth of mildew. Always set storage containers on elevated wood blocks so there is air
   space underneath the containers.
8. Occasionally check stored produce; remove any food that
   looks even slightly spoiled.

Indoor Storage

Indoors you can store food in basements. Select an area away from heating ducts, hot water pipes, and furnaces, because they can raise the temperature of the area you will be using. An ideal spot is near a north corner that has a window for the necessary air circulation. Shade the window so too much light does not enter the area.

Use a basement area of six feet by six feet. The two house-walls will serve as outside walls; build two inner walls of plasterboard or fiberboard nailed to studding. Leave room on one of the two inside walls for a door. Put insulation in the walls you build. Add slatted wood shelves to hold the containers.

Sometimes no construction has to be done in the basement area because there is an existing small storage area, such as an outside entrance to the cellar. This entrance usually has wood or concrete steps under a wide hatch door that is laid at a 45° angle to the ground. The stairwell between the inner door and the hatchway can be a storage spot. You can control temperature by opening the outside hatch to let in cool air or the inside basement door to let in warm air.

Foods to Store

APPLES

Use late-maturing varieties. Pick firm but slightly underripe fruits in the early morning. Discard any apples with blemishes. Do not wash the apples. Store apples in boxes, and use perforated plastic bags or box liners to maintain humidity.

Storage temperature: 32° F.
Humidity: 85 to 90 percent
Length of storage time: several months

BEETS

Use mature but not woody beets. Dig out beets when the soil is dry, and gently brush off the soil from them. Let the beets dry out in a cool place for a few hours so they lose the heat of the soil. Now cut off the tops of the beets to within ½ inch; leave on the tails. Bed the beets in layers of sand in boxes, or store beets in plastic perforated bags.

Storage temperature: 32° to 40° F.
Humidity: 95 percent
Length of storage time: 4 months

CARROTS

Use firm, mature, and unblemished carrots. Rinse or brush them clean and cut off the tops. Store carrots in alternating layers of sand in a box.

Storage temperature: 32° to 40° F.
Humidity: 95 percent
Length of storage time: 4 months

GRAPEFRUITS

Choose firm, unblemished fruits and store them *indoors* only, either unwrapped or wrapped individually. Put the grapefruit in a slatted fruit box.

Storage temperature: 60° F.
Humidity: 95 percent
Length of storage time: 6 to 7 weeks

LEEKS

Pick mature vegetables and use the entire plant, roots and all. Stand the leeks upright in a box and pack them close together. Put soil in around the plants, covering the roots and white parts.

Storage temperature: 32° to 40° F.
Humidity: 95 percent
Length of storage time: 3 months

ONIONS

When onion tops fall over, the vegetables are mature. Once they are mature, onions should rest for a few days in the ground. Then pull up onion plants and cut off the tops to 1 inch above the onion. Put the onions in an airy spot to dry out for a few more days. Store onions in slatted boxes, crates, or mesh bags. Provide excellent air circulation.

Storage temperature: 32° to 35° F.
Humidity: 65 to 75 percent
Length of storage time: several months

PARSNIPS

Dig out parsnips after the first frost. Put them in boxes or crates, and pack sand around them. Parsnips can also be stored in perforated plastic bags.

Storage temperature: 32° F.
Humidity: 95 percent
Length of storage time: 4 to 5 months

PEARS

Pick pears when they are mature and firm; make sure they are unblemished. Harvest as close to freezing weather as possible. Do not wash pears. Put pears in perforated bags and store them in boxes or crates.

Storage temperature: 32° to 35° F.
Humidity: 75 percent
Length of storage time: several months

PEPPERS

Use firm, unblemished peppers, and store them while
they are green. (After they are removed from storage,
they will turn red.) Loosely pack peppers in slatted
boxes or perforated plastic bags. Store *indoors* only.
  Storage temperature: 50° to 54° F.
  Humidity: 95 percent
  Length of storage time: 2 months

POTATOES

When the plant tops start drying out, harvest the pota-
toes. Dig them up carefully so as not to damage them.
Cut potatoes from the plants and store them in boxes or
crates.
  Storage temperature: 40° F.
  Humidity: 95 percent
  Length of storage time: several months

RADISHES

Use winter varieties. Pull up the entire plant and brush
off all dirt. Put radishes in slatted boxes or perforated
plastic bags, or pack them in boxes with moist sand.
  Storage temperature: 32° F.
  Humidity: 95 percent
  Length of storage time: 4 months

RUTABAGAS

Select only unblemished ones. Harvest after frost and
brush off dirt. Cut off tops. Pack rutabagas in sand in
boxes.
  Storage temperature: 32° F.
  Humidity: 95 percent
  Length of storage time: 4 months

SQUASH

Use winter varieties. Remove the fruit from the vine as it matures; leave a 2-inch stem. Keep the squash at average home temperature (78° F.) for a few days. Then, to store, place them side by side, but not touching, in a temperate spot.

Storage temperature: 50° F.

Humidity: 55 percent

Length of storage time: several months

TOMATOES

Use late-maturing varieties. After the first frost, take the tomatoes from the vines and wrap each one in foil. Place tomatoes on shallow trays; do not crowd the fruits. Cover the tomatoes lightly with newspapers. Use *indoor* storage areas only.

Storage temperature: 55° F.

Humidity: 90 percent

Length of storage time: 1 month

TURNIPS

Pull up turnips and cut off the tops; leave ½ inch of the top attached. Brush away any dirt. Put the turnips in a box and pack them with moist sand.

Storage temperature: 32° F.

Humidity: 90 percent

Length of storage time: several months

Remember: do not store fruits and vegetables together. Periodically, sort through all stored vegetables or fruits to see if any are blemished; always remove any blemished fruit immediately.

5 Food Coupon Trading

We have just seen how you can have fresh produce—either by growing it yourself, or by exchanging services for it. Now, what about costly staples like sugar, flour, and so forth? This big question has spawned the great coupon trading movement—and a wise idea it is. It is smart bartering and trading in a big way.

HOW TO DO IT

More and more American manufacturers of food products are offering refunds and cash coupons. You can get orange juice, pizza, peas, pastries, ketchup—you name it. At last count there were something like 7,500 refund offers. Look at any national brands and the chances are they offer a coupon to get refunds or money back. You can save up to $200 a year on your food

budget by paying attention to coupon trades. Of course,
none of this comes without work—you must be organized, or else you end up with mass confusion. But it is
not difficult to keep records and files on your coupons.

Refund forms are found on pads attached to supermarket shelves, in Sunday supplement food advertising
pages, on the products themselves, sometimes inside
the product container, as when you open a jar of Sanka,
and so on. There has always been a problem with coupons: in good times you get a free something you don't
need, and in good times you just disregard it. But in bad
times—no way! Now there are ways of trading coupons. You get rid of those many coupons for dog food
(since you don't have a dog) and swap them with a
neighbor who has excess amounts of coupons for cat
food (since he or she does not have a cat). It all amounts
to saving money.

GETTING STARTED

How do you get in on this great coupon trading revolu-
tion? You can do it by putting up a sign on your supermarket bulletin board saying you will trade coupons. Or
you can start a small neighborhood club in the same
fashion as starting a bartering group—word-of-mouth
inquiries, telephone calls, and so forth, as explained in
Chapter 8.

The biggest and best way to trade coupons is to join
the American Coupon Club—an organization designed
primarily to help consumers save money. The club
gives members special information and services, guid-
ance and support in helping to beat high prices. Annual
membership dues are $15. This entitles you to free clas-

sified ads and refund-form trading letters. You also receive 12 issues of the *National Supermarket Shopper* magazine. Write the American Coupon Club, Dept. BB-1, Box 1149, Great Neck, N.Y. 11023, for further information.

This magazine is the best way of learning of the thousands of refund offers made by manufacturers each year. The offers are arranged in 12 product groups for easy reference. In coupon trading, trades are made in volume—about 20 refund forms at a time. You trade on a one-to-one basis, because you are trading refund forms which are not valuable to you. You might even be sending several $1 refund forms for 50¢ ones. The forms should not be duplicates and must be put in the mail at least 30 days before they expire. Respond promptly.

The American Coupon Club is now chartering local clubs in all parts of the United States. These are called A.C.C. Shoppers' Circles. The club's monthly magazine publishes a list of Shoppers' Circles with name, address, and phone contact for each club. If you want to find out whether there is a Shoppers' Club near you, send a self-addressed stamped envelope to A.C.C. Shoppers' Circle, Dept. BGI, P. O. Box 1149, Great Neck, N.Y. 11023.

If you would rather not join this organization, there are over 1,000 local coupon clubs with no national affiliations. These are neighborhood groups, and you will have to ask around to locate a club. Often your local newspaper may have some information to help you find a refund group.

6 Items You Can Barter

We just discussed food, clothing, and rent—the three major expenditures you should barter for. Here we look at items like antiques, collectibles, used appliances, crafts like pottery and containers, and tools. Also included here is vacation rental trading—a big saving.

This information has been gathered from people who have actually bartered their way to the top by trading these items for other items (or services) they needed and who speak with authority. All these people did the bartering route on a one-to-one basis, without the help of neighborhood groups or national bartering clubs, and so I feel their information is vital to the would-be barterer. (In the next chapter we will discuss bartering services.)

ANTIQUES

This is a field in which you can either lose your head or make a fortune. Antiques are not for everyone, only for those who have a broad education in furniture and the arts and a good idea of the value of things. To go into the antiques field without any knowledge is like trying to operate a roller coaster without safety devices.

Today it seems everyone wants a little piece of yesterday, so antiques, and sometimes even useless junk or used furniture, are excellent bartering material. In fact, bartering is often the only way to get what you want because some collectors will trade, but rarely sell.

Time, experience, and knowledge are necessary if you are to deal in the antiques trade. You must be able to search out and locate those things that you feel will have good potential market value, and this means you must be one step ahead of your competition at auction and house sales.

The qualified antiquer has an inquiring mind and is almost always a shrewd bargainer. Ferret out other areas where antiques exist, such as old store sales, the dumps—*yes,* digging at city dumps—and any business going out of business. Look for house sales and auctions; with an astute mind you might be able to barter a grand piano for an Oriental rug.

Basements and attics are other great places to scrounge around for antiques. When cleaning out an attic in a small town, a friend of mine came across a lovely bird cage. She paid $2 for the cage, but bartered me for some cut flowers worth $20.

COLLECTIBLES

This is a big fad now, encompassing anything from toy soldiers to old advertising tins and cartons. Actually, it is Americana on the loose: old Coca-Cola trays, carnival glass and bottles, comic books, and picture postcards. Collectibles are *not* antiques—antiques are legally at least 100 years old or more. Consider collectibles old (but not antique) nostalgia. With such items you can literally barter yourself into any item you may need desperately. Remember that many collectors will sell their souls to complete a set of baseball cards or a set of miniature furniture.

As in antiquing, you will find collectibles in all sorts of places, from used furniture shops to garage sales to attics and basements. However, you must have an eye for things that will accumulate value in your barter bin. By the way, forget salvage shops and church outlets; the good things have already been picked over long before you get there.

Every year seems to have its fad or trend, and this is what you must watch out for. Try to determine what will be in demand next year, and then go out and look for it and accumulate it. When the trend strikes, you will be holding all the cards and can name your own exchanges. You can trade up, up, and up; really, there is no limit to the profits that can be reaped.

Again, as in most of our pursuits, the collectible route is for those who have the time and knowledge to pursue it, but it is an excellent bartering tool, one that can set you up with many (but not all) of the comforts of life without expending cash.

CRAFTS

The craft explosion of the 1970s was phenomenal. Handmade items became valuable, and today the hand-sewed piece is still highly sought after and prized. You may be a potter, a stained-glass artist, a wire crafter, or a wood carver. There will always be a market for your wares if you are halfway decent at your craft, pursue it diligently, and know how to offer it for trade.

People trained in stained-glass art can practically name their own prices today; whether you are making windows or terrariums, there are people who will seek you out. In return, you can seek them out by asking for things you really need. One stained-glass craftsman I know bartered three windows for an entire year's rent! Another secured her vacation retreat on a free monthly basis in exchange for making a hallway glass mural.

Potters can establish a clientele of customers who in turn refer you to other customers. Haul in your pots and containers twice a month, make your deliveries, and find the exchange pieces you need. There is no middle person, no one to make accounts to, and a happy existence for you.

TOOLS

Bartering with tools may seem farfetched, but it is vir-tually an untapped market. Used tools reconditioned somewhat are as good as new tools these days, and new ones are extremely expensive. Look for old tools—generally they are free merely for the asking. Accumulatethem and then place your ad. You will be surprised at the number of people you can find who are looking for various wood-crafting, carpentry, or gardening tools. The man who furnished me with my garden tools has access to my berry patches for an entire year. I saved hundreds of dollars, and he got huge amounts of vitamins fresh from the vine. (I was quite happy to have someone pick the berries and get rid of them; I had more than enough of them.)

I traded my old skill saw for some plumbing work at my house. I had finished using the saw after ten years and did not think I would have any more use for it. I needed plumbing done in two bathrooms. A trade was struck, and both parties got what they wanted.

Even more of a gold mine—if you have them, or can get them—are *handmade* tools. Such areas of the country as Appalachia, the South, and New England are good sources.

APPLIANCES

Items such as TV sets, refrigerators, ranges, and such can be valuable in bartering, because buying new appliances these days can cost a great deal of money. Many times the old models have a lot of life left in them, and rather than giving the appliance away or trading it in for a new one (where little money is given), you would do well to advertise and find something you want in exchange for that old range or refrigerator.

Further, it seems that a great many people do not

know what to do with old appliances because they are difficult to move, and in most cases the retail store that takes them in exchange for you is the party that makesthe buck. Do it yourself and make a trade. Even appliances that do not work properly represent good dollars and can be repaired even at today's inflationary fees.

FURNITURE

If you are good at crafting furniture, build a supply of small tables, bookcases, and other utilitarian furniture items that people always need. Furniture is expensive these days, with a ridiculous 100 percent markup (sometimes even more)! You can pay as much as $300 for an end table. But you can either build your own or get one from a furniture craftsperson; in either case, you will have furniture with infinitely more charm and value than store-bought items. Besides, today people value handmade items and will be willing to give you in trade more than you think. However, do not price yourself out of the market by asking for too much.

If you yourself do not craft furniture but want some, what would be an equal exchange for, say, a small end table? I would say six hours of typing, a one-day session to photograph a family (to send as Christmas cards), and so on.

Furniture is an excellent bartering tool. Used furniture, however, although worth its value, is not as good. The word "used" always has bad connotations, so the value for a discarded table or bookcase, for example, is not as good as for a hand-crafted piece of furniture.

VACATIONS—HOUSE AND APARTMENT TRADING

Let's say you want to go to Spain for a two-week vacation (maybe Aunt Mary or Uncle Joe gave you the airplane ticket as a gift). Fine. But how do you pay for those expensive hotels? You don't. Instead, trade your apartment or house wherever you live for your accommodations in Spain. House and apartment vacation trading has been popular for many years—it is an ideal way to save that precious cash. You can place classified ads in various magazines offering your living quarters for a place somewhere else. It is a very easy trade to make, and I know dozens of people who have had great vacations and never spent one cent on hotel bills! The price of meals is greatly cut down, as well, because you can do your own cooking.

There are several vacation home exchanges operating in the United States; the largest is Vacation Exchange Club at 350 Broadway, New York, N.Y. 10013. It mails a listing directory every January with a supplement in March. Included are homes in the United States, Canada, Great Britain, Europe, and South America. The directory costs $9 and to make a listing costs $15. Adventures in Living, Box 278, Winnetka, Ill. 60093, is another vacation exchange organization; so is Holiday Home Exchange, at Box 555, Grants, N.M. 87020. Write for current prices and information.

Bartering a vacation place can leave you with extra cash in your pocket that can be put to other important uses. You do not have to support hotels if you would rather not.

7 Services You Can Barter

There are certain talents you may be unaware of that lend themselves to barter; this chapter looks at those skills and talents. Here we will discuss the services that most people can perform in exchange for other services or items.

CHILD CARE AND HOUSEKEEPING

Throughout history people have hired children's nurses and housekeepers. Yet these experts were often relegated to servant status, being considered "of a lower class." Today, however, with mothers working outside the home, everyone is clamoring for good, reliable baby-sitters and efficient housekeepers. Now that the demand is so great, these "servants" can—and do—command fair wages, along with benefits. Thus, many working couples just cannot afford a professional baby-sitter or housekeeper. Here is where bartering can be quite effective. I know a young fellow in my neighborhood who has been very successful bartering such services in exchange for things he needs. In a short time he has acquired an apartment, a houseful of furniture, plants, fresh garden produce, and even an old truck—all acquired by cleaning houses (including washing windows, which no one wants to do). He works only in private homes, not for commercial institutions, and is quite proud of his "profession" and happy with his kind of existence.

If you are at home most of the day and have some free time and genuinely like children, you can find numerous positions. You can, of course, receive wages for child care, but often getting things such as clothing and food in return for services works far better. The wages, because of inflation, disappear quickly at the supermarket, and in the long run you can strike a better bargain trading for things you want. The only prerequisites for child care are a genuine love of children, patience, and the time necessary to do it, and do it properly.

CARPENTRY

If you are skilled at carpentry, you can practically write your own ticket in the barter world. Professional carpenters today make as much as $25 an hour. However, if you know your tools and woods and how to use them and are able to do minor house alterations and repairs, you can soon secure the necessities of life—from furniture to food. You can determine your own hours, take as many jobs as you want, and hold yourself accountable to no one.

In the past I have hired several self-made carpenters who, although perhaps not the very best at the trade, were sufficiently able to make a bookcase or put in a partition. I "paid" these people with vegetables from my garden, furniture I no longer needed and wanted to get rid of, and houseplants—yes, plants, because they have become increasingly expensive at retail stores and thus make for excellent trading.

GARDENING (DESIGN AND MAINTENANCE)

Reading a few self-help books in this area, having an able body and an inquiring mind can set you up with all the necessities of life for little or no expenditures other than a few tools and a used truck. I know so many people who have mastered this type of work that I would say the chances of success are certainly on your side. Good gardeners and designers are at a premium these days, so you can barter away with this service to your profit.

The main reason this particular training pays off is that today there are few, if any, old-time gardeners around, so the profession as a whole has fallen by the wayside. But—and this is a big but—there are many people with small gardens who want some small help and some small landscaping assistance, help they are having a harder and harder time finding. Thus, would-be barterers should investigate this area to secure their living.

PHOTOGRAPHY

This is not as essential a commodity for bartering as some of the others cited, but it does have its demand. Look for people who might like photos in their work, like writers, schoolteachers, professionals, or simply people who want photos of their family pets. I know a young woman who has devoted herself to pet photography—she runs ads in local papers and accepts items in place of money. She has done very well securing her needs, and at the same time she has perfected her craft.

Almost anyone these days, what with the new cameras that do most of the work for you, can take photographs. It is a matter of having the time to do it and the moxie to get out there and make contact with the public to let them know you are available for doing photography work. If possible, specialize in a specific field: garden photographs, people, pets. Once you make yourself into a specialist, you will get more calls.

Photographers need only a few jobs to elicit testimonials and to show how reliable they are to other people. Certainly some friends would give you a start; then you roll from there. Trading your photography skills for needed items saves bundles of money and puts you in charge of your own income picture.

CATERING

If you can cook decently and have a good deal of time and energy, catering small dinners and parties can open the door to securing many, many things you thought were beyond your scope in today's inflationary market. Good caterers are held in high esteem, and if you opt to be paid in other than today's monetary currency, you can accumulate quite an assortment of worldly goods to make yourself self-sufficient and content for some time to come.

Once again, as in most of our bartering skills, catering requires time because it is almost a full-time program. But it can be an enjoyable one—far better than working in a restaurant or even owning one. Caterers can, by working only a few days or nights a week, secure their basic needs without much effort, and in doing so enjoy a great deal of surplus food.

PAINTING

If you ever called a painting contractor to get quotes for painting your home (inside or out), you probably got a terrible shock: the prices make one want to go through the roof! And it is all so expensive because painters' wages average $14 to $20 an hour. If you have your own time and labor to spend and are reasonably agile, you can paint, and in the doing become as professional as any other painter in the world. House painting is basically applying paint to a brush and then applying the brush to a surface. With some practice almost anyone can paint.

If you opt for painting as a bartering medium, doors will open all along the way because no one wants to pay the exorbitant going rates professional painters command these days. And once you have two or three happy clients under your belt, you are off and running.

OFFICE WORK/CLERICAL WORK

General office and clerical help is in tremendous demand today, as evidenced by the want ads in any paper you pick up. If you do typing or other secretarial work out of your own home, you can pick the jobs, the time, and, if you do a reasonably good job within a short period, accumulate a list of clients who will make your life very comfortable. You can easily barter your services here for a multitude of things and/or other services you may require.

SKILLED SERVICES

Electricians, plumbers, and heating experts literally dictate their own terms and rates, and you—unless you are good at fixing and have time for it—must pay. If you are talented in these areas, you can almost name what you want, from furniture to groceries to jewelry. No one really wants to pay $40 an hour to any person for fixing a sink tap or a toilet, putting a fuse in a box, repairing a light fixture, or making a minor repair on a TV or a stereo. So, the man or woman who has mastered these skills is very much in demand. Just put your notice in the local supermarket or local paper to see how right I am.

Note: On skills and trades: painting, carpentry, and so forth—be sure you have liability insurance if you are

trading actively in these areas. It is for your own pro-
tection and for those you trade with.

HOUSE-SITTING

For many years before bartering came into its own,
house-sitting had been an accepted practice, especially
in northern California. This unique trading device is
now practiced in all parts of the country, and there are
professional house-sitters. This is a boon to people who
must be away from home for lengthy periods of time,
because, of course, burglary is always possible in a
house that is empty for many weeks.

The house-sitter is generally a person who may live
in a small city apartment and welcomes the idea of having a vacation in a large house in a rural setting. No
money is exchanged—the owner gets the safety of having someone in his home while he is gone, and the "sitter" gets a lovely vacation. Usually, some sort of gift
—something the sitter wants—is also included in the
trade.

In such a trade it is important to really know who is
going to stay in your home or apartment, and this generally comes from word-of-mouth advertising. However, recently, I have noticed that there are some
individuals who advertise in classified sections of local
papers. These are house-sitters who offer references
and credentials so you can easily check on them to be
sure they are honest and reliable. So if you have no
friend around who can house-sit for you, check out
classified sections as noted, in both newspapers and
magazines.

PROFESSIONAL SERVICES

We have talked a good deal about general things you can do in the bartering arena, but we have not said anything about professional services. Yet doctors, lawyers, architects, dentists, and psychologists charge hefty fees (generally far and beyond what the average person can afford), but in the case of medical aid there are times when it is absolutely necessary. Is it possible to barter for these services? You bet it is! Doctors and dentists (generally being in high-income brackets) are well aware of the tax advantages of making an exchange. They are selling time; it is their time that is so expensive, and a dentist, for example, would much rather have one of his qualified patients design his office or add a room to his home—someone he knows and is working on—than search for a competent designer/architect or carpenter, who can take weeks to find. The human exchange is very important, as well, and works for both parties involved—each will want to do his best when no money is exchanged.

I know an architect who designed his dentist's office in exchange for one year of free dental care for his family of four. How were the values arrived at? Difficult to determine; each person just did some horse trading and struck a deal—you cannot say one service is worth $29 an hour, another $30. A mutual agreement must be struck.

Another dentist bought a house, and the grounds around it needed landscaping. Sure enough, one of his patients was a landscape architect and was more than happy to exchange his professional landscape abilities in trade for dental services for his family and himself;

at the time he was having several teeth capped—a very expensive procedure.

Doctors are quite knowledgeable about bartering, too. My first experience came when I was seeking an introduction to a sport book I had written and needed a few pages about the medical aspects of exercise. When I asked my doctor for some words of wisdom, he was agreeable and in the same breath mentioned he was putting together a lengthy article for a medical journal. Could I perhaps look over his article for editorial content in exchange for the few pages I wanted for my work? He had initiated the barter himself, and I was delighted to save a consultant fee in cash which came out of my pocket, not the publisher's.

Many doctors are collectors of paintings, sculpture, or investment art. If you are an artist of any stature, suggest paying your doctor's bill with a painting. I know this works, as an artist friend has engaged in this type of swapping.

Within the medical field itself, trading services is well established. A doctor cares for the children of a veterinarian in exchange for the vet taking care of the kids' horse if there is a problem. Also, generally no fees are paid when one doctor is ill and seeks professional aid from another doctor. This common courtesy is really nothing more than barter.

So within the medical arena—doctors, dentists, etc. —do seek to barter. They often look for:

- Architectural help
- Landscape architecture aid
- Art commodities, like paintings or sculpture
- Interior design
- Luxury items, like hot tubs, swimming pools, etc.

ACCOUNTANTS; LAWYERS

If you are in business, you need bookkeeping and accounting services which can be expensive. If you have a small business, a full-time person is not necessary, but you need part-time professional help. Why not offer to trade your commodity—what you sell—for such services? Most accountants will latch on to this type of exchange. Make the offer.

Accountants and bookkeepers need various kinds of help—from designing their offices, to having stationery designed and printed, to securing general office help. Try to find something they are looking for and offer them your services.

If you are skillful at bartering, you may even be able to exchange your services for the tax preparation fee that comes yearly.

EDUCATION

One of the most overlooked areas in bartering is education. Many people speak a foreign language, and teaching Spanish or German or French to someone is a helpful service. In this day of air travel, many doctors, dentists, and other professionals go to Europe, and speaking the language can make a big difference in their trips. It can save them money in a foreign country if they can bargain in the native tongue. It also leads to friendlier relations—a respect for the person in learning their language. There are many advantages here.

If you speak another language, you can barter for

many professional services. Most people rebel at the usual language schoolroom courses—too many students in a class; and the problem of time—getting to and from the school. Thus, your one-to-one tutoring can be quite a marketable skill.

And in the area of education, don't forget musical instruction, whether it be piano or voice or guitar. These services are costly, but most instructors will accept a barter for music lessons. Your services in whatever field may be just what the instructor is looking for.

TUTORING

Tutoring is another good area for bartering. I myself have taught small seminars on writing to members of my neighborhood. The exchange was not in money, but in services. One would-be writer was a photographer, another a capable secretary, and still another a printer. I struck three deals in my writing seminar and was satisfied, as were my students, who were happy to learn the basics of writing. Certainly, there are classes in writing, math, language, and so forth. But you must wait until a specific course is taught, you must register, you must be able to get into a class (many times they are full), you must travel to the school, and so on. In small groups or on a one-to-one basis, instruction becomes easy and pleasurable.

COACHING

Not to be forgotten in the bartering arena are coaching and sports. If you are a good tennis, soccer, or racquetball player, for example, consider trading your coaching services. There are a host of people out there who want to learn these sports; make an offer of your services and see what happens.

REAL ESTATE SERVICES

If you are selling a house, there is a commission to the realtor—this may be five percent or more, or may be negotiable, depending upon the state you live in. If you are selling a $100,000 house, the real estate fee can be quite heavy. Many times the broker will accept a trade for partial payment, at least. You may be able to design his garden, help him write a book, or exchange a painting. You can also offer services such as designing graphics for his office, supplying new carpeting or providing furniture, and so on, depending upon your business. And since the fee is negotiable, bartering is a natural extension in this case. Use it and save the money.

ARCHITECTS; INTERIOR DESIGNERS

Architectural services and design consultation are costly, and yet these professional services are needed by many people when building or designing a home, exterior and interior. Few people, however, want to pay the $50-an-hour rate, or whatever it is, so bartering here can reap vast rewards for you. Do you have something an architect might want or that an interior designer would trade services for? Most likely, yes.

Offer your own specialized service—be it painting or

sculpting, remodeling, digging a garden, or trading vegetables. A year's worth of produce at store prices would indeed be quite sufficient for several hours of architectural or design services. Or if you are in a professional arena—lawyer, doctor, etc.—the trade should be easy and big bucks can be saved. Everyone profits, and no money ever need change hands.

The interior designer mentioned in Chapter 2 successfully bartered her services for, as mentioned, her kitchen appliances, in addition to homemade furniture and weekends in a summer house that she later designed for the appliance dealer.

WRITERS; EDITORS

As a very solid case in point of trading services, let me state one of my own experiences. I was offered a contract to do a book on gardening, and the book was to contain many line drawings. My publisher offered to pay a certain advance, but not enough to cover my line-art work. I was not in the position to pay for the line art myself—an expensive commodity these days—so I made an arrangement to trade part of the royalties from the book. The artist was delighted to accept this form of payment.

Writers can also do work for lawyers or doctors or other professionals in many areas.

8 How to Start Your Own Barter Club

Now that you know how to barter, think about starting your own barter club—this can be either a small neighborhood club, or a larger effort. It depends on you, how much time you have, and what kind of organizer you are. Many books have been written on starting your own business, but none of these tells you exactly how to get into the money-saving barter and exchange cycle. It can be done, and it is not that difficult.

Many people now are seeking a different life-style— one that eliminates inflation and excess taxes. These people will want to save themselves money and assure self-sufficiency in the coming years. Barter meets those needs.

Self-sufficiency has a great deal going for it, and in dire times we must fend for ourselves. We must help each other, and going back to the good old-fashioned school of horse trading will help keep us together.

WHAT KIND OF CLUB?

Before you get on the phone or put ads in papers about
your new barter club, select one specific area in which
to barter. It may be crafts or food or services—but
make the specific choice. Follow this guide list to help
you:

1. Make a list of the neighborhood—what kind of people are
   you dealing with?
2. Make a list of their skills or commodities.
3. Do you want a formal or informal organization—neighbors, or people from other regions?
4. Determine values of commodities or services.
5. Determine honesty and willingness of people to share in a
   project.

Let us say you decide on a small, informal neighborhood club—one you can handle easily on a part-time
basis (perhaps three days a week). When you are
screening your members by phone or by letter, ask
them the following questions that will help you determine their possibilities as potential bartering people:

1. Do they like people?
2. Are they willing to share?
3. Have they loaned things out previously on a neighborly
   basis?
4. Do they shop at a good co-op, or would they?
5. Have they ever done any trading or swapping before?
6. What are their thoughts on inflation?
7. Would they be willing to try a barter club for a trial period?

If they have answered five out of the seven questions
affirmatively, chances are they would make excellent
candidates for the club.

GET IT TOGETHER

Once you have your prospective members and have made file cards including name, address, phone, services to offer, and goods to trade, invite everyone to an introductory meeting. This should be easy to do because with gasoline being so costly, many people are staying home more and looking for new activities. Don't make the group too large—20 or 30 people will work fine. At the meeting explain the advantages of bartering. The main thrust of course is exactly what we have discussed previously: to save money. A valid second feature would be to point out the advantages of people working with people. Today many people are more willing to work with their neighbors than, say, five years ago, when everyone felt cozy and secure. While it is true that misery may love company, a group united can do much to erase each other's financial miseries.

Your club can simply operate on a one-to-one basis or referral system, and no one keeps track of the bartering. Each individual is responsible for his or her own transaction. An alternative system is to make your club similar to an exchange, where there is a central record of deposits and withdrawals of labor, services, or skills. This operates much like a bank, with the deposit-and-withdrawal system method. Participants accrue credits by doing things or supplying things, and they use up their credit by receiving services of other members.

In the barter-bank idea, someone must keep the books: the records of transactions made or the credit-debit sheets. The job could be done by one person who would be reimbursed for it by credits. If the club is a barter bank, you will have to have some way of distributing the information—lists of people and what they have to trade or exchange. A simple newsletter sent out monthly will be adequate, or a phone system works well, too, with each member taking a turn each month. For each club member keep a file card that lists name, phone, address, skills, time available, needs, and special talents.

Any community effort will require some money. Expenses for phoning (this can't be avoided) and for stationery supplies will have to be met. These expenses can be paid by charging minimal membership dues.

ESTABLISHING VALUES

Putting the value on labor against services is a major stumbling block in any conversation or in the organization of the barter club. Some member might feel that an hour of his skilled labor is worth more than an hour of a specific service performed by another member. Before you proceed one step further, you must establish a value system.

The easiest way to do this is to operate on the basis that all labor is equal, or on a one-to-one basis. An hour of your typing is equal an hour of baby-sitting, or one piece of furniture is equivalent to another piece of furniture. To avoid complaints with this system, arrange in your club rules that the cost for all equipment used for a job—film, cost of paper, etc., for photography, for example—should be reimbursed by the person for whom the job is done. An electrician would be compensated with money for costs of wire, plugs, etc. If you can agree on this concept, a great deal of bookkeeping and value haranguing will be avoided.

Once your small club is running well, you may find dozens of people who want to join. Beware! And don't allow it to get too big. This could break the back of a good, small, joint neighborhood effort. Instead, help these other people to establish their own barter club in their own area which you could call on when needed, and vice versa. Create a network of barter clubs to help everyone.

ON A LARGE SCALE

While I opt for the small bartering club or "bank," the establishment of the large exchange can work, too. It has advantages because it can offer more in services, such as professional skills of doctors, lawyers, and so forth, as well as small-business participation. There would be a greater variety to be exchanged in goods and services. In a nonprofit large network or exchange, you will be able to reach all kinds of people in all areas —students and the elderly, rather than only neighbors.

A group such as this is fine, but it cannot be handled in spare time or off hours; it needs a firm, tight organization to make it work, plus one very responsible person to lead the way. Perhaps that person is you. However, unlike the small club, which can be started quickly and without much time, the larger exchange will need funding, a board of directors, a membership chairman, articles of democratic laws, a very complete set of trades and exchanges in all areas, and someone with monetary skills to determine the value of each exchange.

If this concept interests you, try to involve an attorney you know well, in addition to one individual who has had training in the business world. The large exchange must be approached as a business, and its success is shown in organizations now working successfully (many of these are listed at the end of the book). If you can get such a group together, then take care of all the necessary legal matters, like setting up a corporation, securing funds, getting members, and filing articles of values.

In essence, it is starting a business, and it must proceed as one. You will find many good books today advising how to start small businesses of your own. Look into these for additional help in establishing the large barter exchange.

9 How Barter Clubs and Exchanges Work

Large-scale barter clubs (not to be confused with neighborhood barter groups) and trade exchanges are proliferating rapidly as inflation continues to zoom. Both are membership organizations comprised of professionals and business owners who never meet but trade and exchange with each other rather than using money. The clubs' inventories include items ranging from plane tickets to architectural services.

BARTER CLUBS

Recently, trading companies have been organized by professional participants who have goods to exchange. The clubs themselves are profit-oriented—they require membership fees and generally take ten percent commission on each barter.

There are reputable clubs, and, unfortunately, ones that are not too reputable. Of the 100 or so organizations we sent letters to asking for information, many were not traceable, which casts a serious doubt on these companies. The word here is *caution*.

The barter clubs act as clearinghouses for goods available for trade. They keep track of how much is earned or spent through barter (usually by a point or unit system), and take inventory of its members. You can trade units between several barter clubs, thus creating a wide selection of goods.

The success of barter clubs depends upon sizable mailing lists of people with things to trade. These clubs operate in all areas of the United States, doing a large business in trading. They may make arrangements for trading any item from a vacation to a land deal. Usually they operate on these six guidelines:

1. Initial joining fee
2. Directory with names and addresses of members, with lists of goods or services available
3. A ten percent service fee on all transactions
4. Sales tax paid by buyer in cash
5. Records of trades made

If you decide to go the route of the collective barter club, be sure you know what you want and its value. Do not accumulate too much credit, and do not borrow a lot of credit from the club. Check available lists closely, and take advantage of trades, even when you may not need the particular items immediately.

The barter club is a good way of getting around the high cost of goods. Its disadvantage is that you never know whom you are dealing with, since the club is controlled by organizations unfamiliar to you. A barter club is not foolproof, and you could be misled into putting out more than you might gain. If you are thinking of joining a barter club, check it out with active members before you join the club. Make certain the club does publish a directory, one that is kept up to date. Talk to club management before joining; if they are reputable, they will not object to your inquiries. Double-check the organization through the Better Business Bureau in your city.

EXCHANGES

Exchanges are becoming big business; they enable strangers to trade *information* and *services* on a non-profit basis. Most of the exchanges we wrote to did answer, and some seem very active. The organizations list services and record labor done and received. A central office handles all correspondence among members.

One successful exchange is the Hilton Exchange, founded in 1955 in California by M. J. Hilton. Other clubs were formed during the 1960s, but it wasn't until 1969 that the major trade exchanges really got their feet off the ground and started to fly. This was the time when wage and price controls were being talked about, and although the Nixon administration did not invoke them until 1971, newspapers and TV predicted them as the harbinger of inflation.

The exchanges are an organized way for people to trade easily and quickly; you do not have to do the recruiting or the organization. Sophisticated computers do this for the large-scale companies. The exchanges offer information and data on what is available for trading, and they also keep records of what is traded.

Exchanges are now located throughout the United States. The Business Exchange in Los Angeles has 5,000 members and 30 franchises. Exchange Enterprises, located in Arizona, has franchises in many cities. The Columbus Trade Exchange, in Columbus, Ohio, is another example of a successful company.

HOW THEY OPERATE

Exchange Enterprises, established over ten years ago in Salt Lake City, Utah, is a bartering company for business and professional services. The parent company has licensed independently owned offices in some 36 cities in 14 states, and more than 25,000 members barter locally and nationally through the exchanges. Some offices reputedly handle millions of dollars in trades a year.

The company newsletter *Exchanging Times* claims that in 1978 membership and trade volume tripled, sales force and offices tripled, and sophisticated computers have become part of the operation to keep records of negotiations. Basically, these exchanges (whether Exchange Enterprises or any other) are referral and bookkeeping businesses, and one of the main advantages of an exchange is the extra business gained through company referrals. In essence, it acts as its own advertisement. It is possible, so the exchanges say, to increase business by 15 percent without any change in overhead cost.

One reason one member joined an exchange was so that he could trade his goods for travel expenses, car rentals, motel bills, and so forth when he goes on buying trips—thus saving large amounts of cash.

All transactions are made in trade units or scrip, and no cash is involved. There is a membership fee of $25, and annual dues are $350 (this may vary with individual organizations). In general, an exchange contract says that the member agrees to sell his service or product at prevailing prices to other members and pays the company a service charge of ten percent in trade units—not cash—for each purchase. A new member is given a credit card and then the company refers would-be buyers to the business. When the new member accumulates trade credits by providing goods or services, he then can use those units to purchase from other members.

All transactions must go through the exchange and be approved by it. The member makes his purchase with his credit card, the seller sends the invoice slips to the office, the purchaser is debited retail value of the product plus a ten percent service charge plus sales tax, all in trade units. The seller gets credit in trade units for the retail value. Monthly statements are sent to members through the central office.

A successful exchange must maintain a balanced economy so that if one business section becomes filled to accommodate the membership, that area is closed—no more clients are accepted. On the other hand, when there is a business required by members, the sales force actively looks for clients in that area.

Within a specific territory, you can obtain a franchise for an exchange business. This allows you to enlarge the market area by dealing with other members, conserving cash, and obtaining needed products and services. The franchisee can also market his clients' products through a network of other exchanges. The local franchisee can also purchase (on a traded basis) needed products available from other cities, or from a company such as Exchange Enterprises International.

The concept of the exchange can become a huge network operating much in the same way as a national credit card company (like American Express), with one big difference—*no cash is exchanged*. It is even possible with exchanges as clearinghouses to trade services and goods from a manufacturer to a hotel chain to a retailer, and so forth. Giant complexes are possible, and some of these are already forming (see Appendix at back of book for list of exchanges).

Another form of exchange club operating in *services or work* only, rather than *products*, is Work Exchange, in Milwaukee, Wisconsin. This group is well organized, and both young and old participate in trading. Members are recruited by:

1. Door-to-door canvassing
2. Informal sales speeches to older adult groups
3. Public service announcements
4. Local social service groups
5. Posters placed in churches, civic centers, etc.

The new member is interviewed in his or her home by a Work Exchange person. Here, basic information is received and recorded, such as a description of what is needed, what services are offered, some personal references, and signature on release of liability statements —a very important part of this type of concept. The accepted members then receive an identification card and a Work Exchange Policy Statement.

Work trading may be done in such diversified areas as:

• Appliance repair
• Baby-sitting

- Baking and Cooking
- Housecleaning
- Minor home maintenance
- Moving
- Outdoor work

The amount of time which was given in the process of completing various tasks is recorded by the staff, and follow-up phone calls are made to see that everyone was satisfied.

In the course of a year, members have either performed a service, received a service, or both given and received a service at least once.

Give careful thought before joining any network or exchange or barter club and study all literature carefully. As with all membership organizations, don't join unless you really mean to participate and be honest about your skills. Don't try to break the club by commercializing an exchange relationship—hiring the person on your own. Be prepared to be part of the group and help with criticism—these are sharing experiences.

OTHER EXCHANGES

Craftsmen's and collectibles fairs and show co-ops are starting in many rural areas. Here the craftsman brings his wares to trade; you find ads for these shows in local papers and advertisements in the town proper. Mill Valley, California, and Rhinebeck, N.Y., have crafts fairs that boggle the mind, with thousands of people attending. There are other areas, as well, that have these horse trading events.

The Federation of Women's Exchanges sponsors crafts exchanges—to date there are 41 in the United

States. Generally, these exchanges carry handiwork; others offer antiques and foodstuffs, as well. The exchanges usually operate on a 25 percent commission; 75 percent goes to the craftworker. Usually, the craftsperson pays a modest fee per year to join. The New York Exchange for Women's Work started 95 years ago, and more than 1,000 women annually supplement their income this way. The annual membership is $3, and a commission of 5 percent is added to the net price. There is also a 20 percent overhead charge.

The address in New York is:

Woman's Exchange
660 Madison Ave.
New York, N.Y. 10022

You can get a complete list from:

The Women's Bureau
Massachusetts Department of Commerce and Development
100 Cambridge St.
Boston, Mass. 02202

Another organization you may want to join is:

The Elder Craftsman Shop of Philadelphia
Phildadelphia, Penn. 19103

10 Barter and the I.R.S.

The I.R.S. seems to be part of everyone's life; taxes certainly eat into our income. However, barter should never be considered as just a way to avoid paying taxes. You can stay well within the law by paying taxes but still save with bartering. And I strongly suggest that you consult a qualified accountant on your barter exchanges if you barter on a large scale. The following information is general and should in no way be construed as a way to avoid I.R.S. taxes.

RULES OF THE GAME

To the I.R.S., barter constitutes income—income that must be declared and paid for as though you were dealing in cash. Just how you declare it and at what cash value depends on you and your accountant.

To quote verbatim from Section 61A of the Internal Revenue Code:

Except as otherwise provided in the subtitle, gross income means all income from whatever source derived including but not limited to [the following items]. . . .

Barter is not listed among "the following, items," so many people construe this as meaning that barter does not apply. But my tax consultant advises me that barter *is* included, so thus I abide by the rules. Your accountant may have other interpretations—again, this is an individual decision.

However, the I.R.S. code goes on to include the Common Notable Exchange Clause 1031, which deals with the exchange of property held for productive use or investment:

No gain or loss shall be recognized if property held for productive use in trade or business or for investment is exchanged solely for property of a like kind to be held either for productive use in trade or business or investment.

So it seems exchanges are possible in certain areas —property, for example—if exchanged for similar property that is to be held for either use in trade or business or investment. However, once you sell the investment, you must pay capital gains tax.

Other items, such as antiques, trucks, vegetables, or whatever, if traded for items in kind, could mean that taxes are not an issue. Consider the words "in kind" and take it from there on your own—please.

Another nebulous area in the I.R.S. code offers some relief and says:

Income tax does not have to be declared on gifts which are exchanged.

So as you can see, ambiguities exist; what may seem taxable to one I.R.S. person may not seem so to another person, so judge accordingly. Again, I urge you to consult the experts.

Obviously, if you do not report barter as income, it may be difficult to trace. The barterer may have the advantage of eliminating state sales tax, and nontaxable exchange in kind and the nontaxable exchange of gifts are well within the law; let your conscience be your guide. Other barter advantages include not having to pay tax at the time you earn your credit units with an exchange company because: 1. it has not yet been converted to income; and 2. you are operating as a business, trading wholesale for wholesale. In addition, another big advantage of bartering is that you save cash, so declaring values are up to you. Who can really say exactly what an item is worth? That varies from week to week. Judge accordingly.

In general, the I.R.S. is not always the demon people think it is. They are more concerned with people who try to hide large amounts of income rather than people who honestly make errors on deductions. Generally, they tend to ignore small barterers. If you trade 12 squash for 12 tomatoes, this hardly affects your income; similarly, when you trade furniture for furniture, and so forth, the I.R.S. is not likely to be interested. The I.R.S. is more concerned about company or business barterers.

This is the situation today, but it could change by the time this book reaches print. There has been increasing interest in bartering and trading, and although usually no money is exchanged, the exchange of services and items represents—to both parties (and possibly the I.R.S.)—income, and therefore must be reported and is subject to taxation. But—and this is a big but—many barters are deductible as business expenses.

In short, do not cheat. Make fair declarations of trades and exchanges, and above all keep accurate and clear records in case you are called in to explain your bartering practices. The important thing when figuring taxes in barter is not how much you traded, but the fair-market value of what you received in exchange.

It is not sensible or reasonable to risk tax fraud in relation to barter. By bartering you have certain advantages to improve your economic position. Remember the sections involving nontaxable exchange in kind and nontaxable exchange of gifts—this may give you quite an edge in your income tax picture. And, of course, there is also the possible elimination of state sales tax.

The barter boom has caused the I.R.S. to pay more attention to what formerly was regarded as a pesty fly in a restaurant. The restaurant is becoming filled with flies, and thus the I.R.S. is starting to take notice of barter transactions with a more careful eye. The official stand set forth in the guidelines of the I.R.S. revenue ruling is that the value of revenue units received by members of barter clubs "should be included in the gross income of the member income tax for the taxable year in which the credit is acquired."

Individual barter arrangements such as when a doctor does work for an electrician and the electrician rewires the doctor's home in trade should also be taxed according to the dollar value of those services, so says the I.R.S.

However, it is inconceivable for the government to hear about all the individual trades and exchanges. Still, I urge you to keep records of all trades and exchanges and consult with your accountant at tax time to avoid any possible hassles with the I.R.S.

11 One Family's Bartering

All of what you have read may sound good in principle, but you are probably asking yourself just how much you can actually save a year by bartering. Let's look at one typical family's annual effort in bartering in order to get some real figures.

I have selected a family of four, with the husband and wife in their mid-thirties, and two small children. They are essentially sharing people and live in a friendly neighborhood, so bartering came naturally for them and was an easy step toward self-sufficiency. The family is basically very friendly and had a good network of people to work with. They did not join any local clubs or national clubs, but did bartering strictly on a one-to-one basis. This is their record:

1. Received fresh produce all year from a neighbor's garden: value at a supermarket—$400

2. Bartered for 80 percent of their clothing needs from a skilled seamstress in the neighborhood: value at a store—$1,000
3. Secured handmade furniture from a craftsman—a dining table and four chairs, end tables, and two bookcases: value at a store—$1,200
4. Got music lessons for two children: value—$400
5. Got their house painted: value—$700
6. Secured two used bicycles: value—$200
7. Got used garden tools: value—$400
8. Exchanged their house for a vacation rental for three weeks: value—$1,500

In these easily made barters, this family saved close to $6,000 in one year. What did they "give" in return? Mr. Smith is an excellent mechanic and carpenter—most of what they got came from his skills. Mrs. Smith is a housewife with time which she used for baby-sitting, car-pooling, typing, and canning foods for exchange purposes.

It was interesting to note that the Smiths were unable to barter for dental and doctor bills or for an attorney when one was needed. Had they been members of a national exchange, this probably could have been accomplished.

HELPFUL HINTS IN BARTERING

1. Don't be overanxious or overbearing.
2. Decide exactly what you want to barter for and what you have in exchange.
3. Do not discuss price—just items you want in exchange for others you have to offer.
4. Never downgrade the value of an item being offered for barter—either you can or cannot use it.

5. Don't make irrational offers, such as asking for a grand piano in exchange for a bushel of zucchini.
6. If arguments about values—of services or goods—arise, abandon the barter; otherwise, there will always be repercussions.
7. When the trade is made, be sure everyone is satisfied.
8. Don't renege on the deal; if worst comes to worst and you don't want the item, trade it off elsewhere later.
9. Keep phone contacts for future bartering.
10. Offer to trade this book (after you have read it, of course) for another book.

12 When Push Comes to Shove

In this book we have extolled the value and advantages of barter as a life-style and a means to beat inflation (or at least keep up with it). We have suggested ways of bartering to help you supplement an income and help to keep your cash in your pocket. But what happens if price controls and general chaos explode in the near future? In other words, what will you do if there is a crash. If you know how to barter—and hopefully you do by now—you will survive while those around you will flounder.

In dire days and bad times, and if rationing becomes effective for various commodities (as it might with gasoline), there is an economic breakdown and the monetary unit becomes almost worthless. Bartering becomes paramount. And the basics you have learned in bartering for food, clothing, shelter, and so forth take on added and very important dimensions in how you survive. Certain items will demand more than others in bad times; certain skills will be necessary to survive in a rationed world.

BEST COURSE OF ACTION

If push comes to shove, start by storing food; in a truly serious world condition, food actually functions as currency. You will need extra food beyond your own use with which to barter. Know how to grow and store food as we explained in Chapter 4.

Treasure those used tools I mentioned in previous chapters because repairs of all kinds will be in high demand. Stockpile any extra tools—they can be fodder for bartering for essentials. Tools are also important for self-sufficiency.

Collect clothing of all kinds—from shoes to hats to everyday wearing apparel; these are essential and make good bartering wares.

Start accumulating everyday necessities, like soap, toilet paper, light bulbs, and so on.

If you feel you are hoarding, you are not; you are merely preparing yourself for bartering in a survival situation. And since most of what you have stockpiled has been accumulated from trading, you could hardly be called down for hoarding.

In bad times, food, clothing, and tools (in addition to skills) are the passwords to survival, and that is why I implore you to read Chapter 4 again and get on the bandwagon. Once rationing starts, it will be too late.

WHEN THE BOOM FALLS

When the government starts rationing necessities, you will receive ration coupons for many commodities. Some of us remember them well from World War II times. I do, and living with rationing is no joke. There is never enough of anything to go around, and obviously black-marketing becomes rampant. It is not a very happy world to live in.

If you are an experienced barterer and have prepared yourself, you need not worry about black-marketing or ration coupons. Once ration coupons appear you will have to trade them, and if you know how to barter you have a head start. You will be in the driver's seat because in a ration society things can get into a panic state. In time, if controls have not been broken down or thrown off, crime soars, government tightens grips on urban cities, and money becomes worthless. Although ration coupons are on hand, they, too, may actually mean very little. Barter is everything.

Strikes and breakdowns in municipal services are common (they already have occurred in many cities), and misery becomes rampant—look at photos of the Great Depression of the 1930s and you'll know it is possible. You will have to barter to live decently.

If I sound like a doomsday forecaster, consider the following:

There was a bread strike some two years ago and no bread was on supermarket shelves for several days. When the first shipment finally arrived after the strike ended, people literally knocked down their neighbors to get that bread.

In a truckers' strike in California some years back when word got out that commodities would be in short-supply, scores of housewives and househusbands almost tore down the doors to supermarkets and literally cleaned out shelves of sugar, flour, and other necessary everyday staples.

And in the time of shortages such as the coffee debacle, I remember you could not find a can of coffee for love or money. Even the man with gold coins wouldn't be able to buy any if there was none available. But the smart barterer would have had some coffee stashed away—he could well get that gold coin.

The list of panic situations could be accentuated over and over again, but it is enough to say that in bad times things do happen—and they are not good things. Everyone wants to survive, and it's only natural to want food to survive. It is simply a facet of human nature.

YOU'VE GOT—I HAVEN'T

What if you have been a smart trader. You are prepared with a good supply of foods and tools and commodities necessary for everyday living. Suddenly hell breaks loose and things start to go down the tubes? Doesn't this put you in a vulnerable position? Or, to be succinct: Isn't it likely that if you have when others do not, they will try to take your food away by any means (at gunpoint, for instance)? I doubt very much if this would happen. Even in times of famine—while there was some theft, some looting—mobs of hungry citizens acting like wild packs of wolves still did not appear at one's doorstep. On the other hand, I would never advertise that *there was food available* at my home.

And, hopefully, I would live in a neighborhood where most people are familiar with bartering, have practiced it, and would have their own small emergency supplies to tide them over the bad times. At least they would if they had read this book.

APPENDIX
Barter and Exchange Organizations

These organizations either engage in barter or exchange—some for skills, others labor, others professional services, and still several others suggesting alternative life-styles in which cash is not paramount. This list is by no means complete, and an organization's inclusion does not imply the author's endorsement. Look completely into the workings of any organization (whether listed or unlisted) before joining. Also, inquire in your own community as to the existence of other organizations.

NORTHEAST/EAST

AMERICAN BARTER SYSTEMS
Division of Area Barterers, Inc.
170 East Post Road
White Plains, N.Y. 10601

AMERICAN COUPON CLUB
Dept. BB-1, Box 1149
Great Neck, N.Y. 11023

This is one of the large coupon trading clubs for food, and it's a very successful one, with thousands of members. Annual dues are $12. It offers a magazine and valuable publications; it trades coupons only.

AMERICAN RECIPROCAL TRADE SYSTEMS, INC.
9 Northern Boulevard
Greenvale, N.Y. 11548

AMERICAN RECIPROCAL TRADE SYSTEM, INC.
95 Madison Avenue
New York, N.Y. 10016

BARTER AMERICARD
2973 Bond Drive
Merrick, N.Y. 11566

BARTERTOWN
476 Broadway
New York, N.Y. 10013
(212) 964-4190

CENTRAL PENNSYLVANIA TRADE EXCHANGE
2233 N. Front Street
Harrisburg, Pa. 17105

CONNECTICUT TRADE EXCHANGE
700 Burnside Avenue
East Hartford, Conn. 06108

DELAWARE VALLEY TRADE
1150 1st Avenue #410
King of Prussia, Pa. 10506

EVERYTHING FOR EVERYBODY
298 Columbus Ave.
Boston, Mass. 02116
(617) 262-6634

This exchange service deals in work and provides a perpetual free market. There are three locations in New York, as well. Membership is $5 a month, or $100 for life.

INTERNATIONAL INDEPENDENCE INSTITUTE
Robert Swan
639 Massachusetts Ave.
Cambridge, Mass. 02139
(617) 661-4661

This works on a commodity-based currency. Creative economic thinking goes on here.

INTERNATIONAL TRADE EXCHANGE
7656 Burford Drive
McLean, Va. 22101
(703) 821-1101

KENTUCKY TRADE EXCHANGE
129 Briarwood Road
Versailles, Ky. 40383

THE MAINE TRADE EXCHANGE
980 Forest Avenue
Portland, Me. 04103

NEW ENGLAND TRADE EXCHANGE
1 Padanaram Road 115
Danbury, Conn. 06810

NEW HAMPSHIRE TRADE EXCHANGE
RFD 1, Box 151
Auburn, N.H. 03032

PHILADELPHIA TRADE EXCHANGE
Doyle Building, Route 130
Burlington, N.J. 08016

PITTSBURGH TRADE EXCHANGE
471 Lincoln Avenue
Pittsburgh, Pa. 15202

PORTLAND TRADE EXCHANGE
980 Forest Avenue
Portland, Me. 04103

PRINCETON CENTER FOR ALTERNATIVE FUTURES, INC.
60 Hodge Rd.
Princeton, N.J. 08540
(609) 921-2280
   This is a good resource center for books written on economics that include bartering as a possible alternative.

ROCHESTER TRADE EXCHANGE
16 West Main Street #438
Rochester, N.Y. 14614

TRADE EXCHANGE OF NEW JERSEY
77 Milltown Road
East Brunswick, N.J. 08816

TRI-CITY TRADE EXCHANGE
1985 Central Avenue
Albany, N.Y. 12205

TRI-STATE TRADE EXCHANGE, INC.
603 Fairway Drive
West Chester, Pa. 19380

VACATION EXCHANGE CLUB
350 Broadway
New York, N.Y. 10013
(212) 966-2576
   This club furnishes the *Home Exchange Directory*, which describes your home and its particulars along with similar details of thousands of other homes being offered for exchange during the year. Subscription costs range from $9 to $15, depending on what time of year and with which supplement you are getting the directory. The directory contains more than 2,000 addresses from all over the world.

WESTERN NEW YORK TRADE EXCHANGE
3095 Elmwood Avenue
Town of Tonawanda, N.Y. 14217

WORCESTER TRADE EXCHANGE
57 Cedar Street
Worcester, Mass. 01609

SOUTH

ARK-LA-TEX TRADE EXCHANGE
P.O. Box 5763
Shreveport, La. 71105

CENTRAL FLORIDA TRADE EXCHANGE
508 Orange Drive #2
Altamonte Springs, Fla. 32701

CHARGE-A-TRADE
3081 East Commercial Blvd.
Fort Lauderdale, Fla. 33308
(305) 491-2700
   This is a business-oriented barter club that uses the credit-card system and computers to keep track of exchanges.

EAST TENNESSEE EXCHANGE
P.O. Box 26
Sweetwater, Tenn. 37874

GREATER ATLANTA TRADE EXCHANGE
2219 Perimeter Center East
Atlanta, Ga. 30346

GULF COAST TRADE EXCHANGE
P.O. Box 8125
Pensacola, Fla. 32505

IMA CORPORATION/ABBA FOUNDATION
628 Frenchman St.
New Orleans, La. 70116
(504) 954-3340

A group of alternative businesses earn money to provide their foundation with funds for community services. Many of the businesses are open to barter. In general, skills are more valued than money.

ITE OF BROWARD COUNTY/PALM BEACH
2440 East Commercial Blvd.
Ft. Lauderdale, Fla. 33310

JACKSON TRADE EXCHANGE
1755 Lelia Drive #102
Jackson, Miss. 39216

LAKE CHARLES TRADE EXCHANGE
P.O. Box 5915
Lake Charles, La. 70606

NASHVILLE TRADE EXCHANGE
No. 2 Maryland Farms #339
Brentwood, Tenn. 37027

NATIONAL COMMERCE EXCHANGE
6091 Loisdale Road
Springfield, Va. 22150

NEW ORLEANS TRADE EXCHANGE
7303 Downman Road
New Orleans, La. 70126

SOUTH CAROLINA TRADE EXCHANGE
P.O. Box 12452
Columbia, S.C. 29211

TRADE EXCHANGE OF NORTH CAROLINA
926 Second Street N.E.
Hickory, N.C. 28601

VIRGINIA TRADE EXCHANGE
1631 Old Virginia Beach Rd. #B
Virginia Beach, Va. 23453

MIDWEST

ARKANSAS TRADE EXCHANGE
11121 North Rodney Parham
Little Rock, Ark. 72212

BUSINESS OWNERS' EXCHANGE
4901 W. 77th St.
Minneapolis, Minn. 55435
(612) 835-2233
    This is a business barter group claiming to have turned
over $1,000,000 in trade in 1976. There is a $150 joining fee
and dues of $25 a year.

CINCINNATI TRADE EXCHANGE
11413-A Century Blvd.
Cincinnati, Ohio 45246

COLUMBUS TRADE EXCHANGE
7870 Olentagny River Rd.
Columbus, Ohio 43085
(614) 846-4041
    This is a large organization that operates in various areas
of trades and barter—professional services and businesses
being the main thrust. Franchises are available. Write for full
data.

COMMON GROUND CRISIS CENTER
1090 South Adams
Birmingham, Mo. 93130
(313) 645-9676
    This is a center specializing in lists of talents and skills
which include barter and trade.

DAYTON TRADE EXCHANGE
1150 Richfield Center Rd.
Dayton, Ohio 45430

GREATER IOWA TRADE EXCHANGE
Equitable Building #812
Des Moines, Iowa 50309

ITE OF EASTERN OHIO & WESTERN
PENNSYLVANIA
821 Dlooar Bank Bldg.
Youngstown, Ohio 44503

ITE OF INDIANA
537 Turtle Creek S. Dr. # 10
Indianapolis, Indiana

ITE OF OMAHA
5717 Hickman Road
Des Moines, Iowa 50310

LEARNING EXCHANGE
Carol (Maura) Berk-Fonte
Ann Arbor, Mich.
(313) 599-1447

THE LEARNING EXCHANGE
P. O. Box 920
Evanston, Ill. 60204
(312) 273-3383

These groups trade close to 3,000 different items and services among 30,000 participants. Registration fee is $15 per year regular, $7.50 per year limited-income membership. Details of terms of trade are left to the barter parties.

MICHIGAN TRADE EXCHANGE
29246 Van Dyke
Warren, Mich. 48093

MIDWEST TRADE EXCHANGE
2650 N. Lakeview Dr. #2701
Chicago, Ill. 60614

NORTHERN ILLINOIS TRADE EXCHANGE
1806 South Alpine
Rockford, Ill. 61108

TOLEDO TRADE EXCHANGE
121½ West Indiana Ave.
Perrysburg, Ohio 43551

WICHITA TRADE EXCHANGE
8210 North Oliver
Valley Center, Kans. 67147

WORK EXCHANGE INC.
2201 N. 35th St.
Milwaukee, Wisc. 53208
(414) 445-4786
This is an organization for labor and work exchange operating mainly in a specific area; it includes skilled and nonskilled work duties.

WEST

CALIFORNIA PUBLIC POLICY CENTER
304 South Broadway
Los Angeles, Calif. 90013

or

1434 Westwood Blvd.
Los Angeles, Calif. 90024
(213) 628-8888, or (213) 474-4518
This organization provides community groups with listings of individuals who can assist in alternative economic policies and research information about the economic development in our country now.

EXCHANGE ENTERPRISES
159 Haven Ave.
Salt Lake City, Utah 84115
(801) 487-1641

This is a business barter club with franchises around the country.

FREE SIG
1623 Grandville Ave.
11-P,
Los Angeles, Calif. 90025
(213) 826-9665

This is a labor cooperative consisting of 100 members. A monthly update of new members and their skills and a status report on old members are published. A $5 registration fee is required. This is a nonprofit labor co-op.

HILTON EXCHANGE
5032 Lankershim Blvd.
North Hollywood, Calif. 91601
(213) 877-3681

This group has been in business more than 25 years. There is no monthly service directory or statements—just tell them what you need. It's $175 for the first year, $50 annual dues in cash. There is no minimum service charge, but ten percent in trade for transactions. This group is mostly 100 percent barter.

MUTUAL CREDIT
6300 Variel St.
Woodland Hills, Calif. 93167
(213) 703-6500

Offices throughout the United States.

NORTH AMERICAN TRADE EXCH. OF DENVER, INC.
6850 East Evans Avenue
Suite 140
Denver, Colo. 80224

TRADE NOTE INTERCHANGE
819 Eleventh Avenue
Delano, Calif. 93215

UNITED TRADE CLUB
3031 Trisch Way
San Jose, Calif. 95100

UNLIMITED BUSINESS EXCHANGE
3471 South West Temple
Salt Lake City, Utah 84115

INSTITUTE FOR THE STUDY OF ALTERNATIVE
LIFE-STYLES—COLLECTIVE RESEARCH COMPANY
P. O. Box 1125
Rohnert Park, Calif. 94928
(707) 795-1556

LA COALICIÓN SERVICE CENTER
260 Rodriguez
Watsonville, Calif. 95076
  This organization uses labor exchange under the auspices
of the Service Center.

SELF DETERMINATION—A PERSONAL/POLITICAL
NETWORK
P. O. Box 126
Santa Clara, Calif. 97052
(408) 984-8134

TRADEAMERICARD
777 South Main St.
Orange, Calif. 92668
(714) 543-8283
  A quarterly newsletter is published; so are a dining and
entertainment guide, plus a monthly directory. There are four
member get-togethers a year. Reciprocal contacts exist in
San Francisco, Hawaii, Florida, and Mexico.

BARTER SYSTEMS OF SAN MATEO
25 Edwards Court
Suite 210
Burlingame, Calif. 94010

BUSINESS EXCHANGE OF NORTHERN CALIFORNIA
41580 Fremont Blvd.
Fremont, Calif. 94538

BUSINESS EXCHANGE, INC.
International Headquarters
4716 Vineland Ave.
North Hollywood, Calif. 91602
(213) 877-2161 or 984-1233
    Mammoth organization with dozens of franchises through-
out United States.

BLUE KEY EXCHANGE
Wells Fargo Bank Building, Suite 416
851 Burlway Rd.
Burlingame, Calif. 94010

UNITED TRADE CLUB
3575 Stevens Creek Blvd., Suite G
San Jose, Calif. 95117

TRADE SYSTEMS CORP.
1777 Saratoga Ave., Suite 200
San Jose, Calif. 95129

COMSTOCK TRADING COMPANY
P. O. Box 8020
Walnut Creek, Calif. 94596

NORTHWEST

CASCADIAN REGIONAL LIBRARY INFORMATION
ACTION CLEARINGHOUSE
454 Willamette
P. O. Box 1492
Eugene, Ore. 97401
(503) 485-9430

COMMUNITY ENERGY BANK
32250 Fox Hollow Rd.
Eugene, Ore. 97405
(503) 342-0284
   This is a nonprofit service exchange dealing in labor credits
and debits. Exchanges occur one-to-one or on the basis of
credit hours, or combine credit hours and money.

COMMUNITY ENERGY BANK
Kathy Bing
41 Third Street
Ashland, Ore. 97520
   This is a nonprofit service exchange.

NORTHWEST TRADE NETWORK
Halsey Brant
P. O. Box 1108
White Fish, Mont. 59937
   This is a network to link the various collective and labor
coops in the Northwest area.

PEOPLE'S TRANS SHARE
Portland, Ore.
(503) 227-2419
   This group was founded by Joe Bentivegna. It is a nation-
wide transportation service with 8,200 members. There is a
$10-a-year for ride referrals. Members must answer a per-

sonal questionnaire, be 17 or older to register. "P.T.S. does not get people rides. We simply provide the information referral service."

SERVICE EXCHANGE
3534 Southeast Main St.,
Portland, Ore. 97214
(503) 232-0543, or (503) 232-7335

SOUTHWEST

EXCHANGE ENTERPRISES
4625 E. Fort Lowell #205
Tucson, Ariz. 85712
(602) 881-5688

2328 West Campus
Tempe, Ariz. 85282
(502) 894-2367
   This is a large organization dealing in all types of services and businesses—it has branches or franchises in many cities. It operates on a card system. It's well organized and claims thousands of members.

DALLAS/FT. WORTH TRADE EXCHANGE
5019 N. McKinney #130
Dallas, Tex. 75205

HIGH PLAINS TRADE EXCHANGE
724 S. Polk Street #901
Amarillo, Tex. 79101

SAN ANTONIO TRADE EXCHANGE
6836 San Pedro Road South #105
San Antonio, Tex. 78216

WEST TEXAS TRADE EXCHANGE
7212 Joliet Street #3-B
Lubbock, Tex. 79423

WESTERN TRADE EXCHANGE
1855 Trawood Avenue #E
El Paso, Tex. 79935

Suggested Reading

The Ruff Times, P.O. Box 2000, San Ramon, Calif. 94583; $145 per year

Gary North's Remnant Review, P.O. Box 35547, Phoenix, Ariz. 85069; $60 per year

Daily News Digest, P.O. Box 39027, Phoenix, Ariz. 85069; $125 per year; 5-week trial, $15

Personal Finance Letter (formerly *Inflation Survival Letter*), P.O. Box 2599, Landover Hills, Md. 20784; 24 issues, $54

The ABC's of Home Food Dehydration, Barbara Densley, Horizon Publishing; $3.95

Making the Best of Basics, James Talmage Stevens, Peton Corporation; $5.95

Let's Try Barter, Charles Morrow Wilson, Devin-Adair Publishing; $4.95

How to Prosper During the Coming Bad Years, Howard Ruff, Warner Books; $2.75

How You can Profit From the Coming Price Controls, Gary North, American Bureau of Economic Research (write for price)

1980 Guide to Coupons and Refunds, Martin Sloane, Bantam Books; 1980;

Cashing in at the Checkout, Stonesong Press; 1979;

Note: Don't buy all of these—buy one or several, and trade off with friends for others.